Living
Learning
Leadership

Gaile O. Newsome

ISBN 979-8-89112-079-2 (Paperback)
ISBN 979-8-89112-080-8 (Digital)

Copyright © 2024 Gaile O. Newsome
All rights reserved
First Edition

All rights reserved. No part of this publication may be reproduced, distributed, or transmitted in any form or by any means, including photocopying, recording, or other electronic or mechanical methods without the prior written permission of the publisher. For permission requests, solicit the publisher via the address below.

Covenant Books
11661 Hwy 707
Murrells Inlet, SC 29576
www.covenantbooks.com

CONTENTS

ACKNOWLEDGMENT

All glory, honor, and praise to the Almighty God, my Lord and Savior, Jesus Christ. With the Lord's help and guidance, I have arrived at this station and season of my life. Praise God.

I feel blessed to have had the parents that were so precious in my life, Bishop Everett C. Newsome I and Rev. Dr. Olga G. Newsome. Through them, a strong spiritual foundation helped shape my life.

Although our scholastic experience has been redesigned because of life experiences, I have greatly benefited from all that I have received from the New Greater Bethel Bible Institute. May the Lord continue to bless the entire staff and faculty and their ministry of nurturing. Amen.

INTRODUCTION

He shall feed his flock like a shepherd: he shall gather
the lambs with his arm, and carry them in his bosom,
and shall gently lead those that are with young.
—Isaiah 40:11

Leadership is an inexhaustible subject. Whether it references a position, an ability, an act, a function, an instance, or a group, it usually deals with who has the final say or how a specific entity is to proceed. The initial inclination that arises when the subject of leadership is spoken of is to look at or for the leader. Who are they? How do they look? How do they act? Where did they come from? Where can you, did you, do you find them? Are they present in body, in thoughts, and in alertness? All of this is involved and is sometimes assessed in the first impression. This individual, who carries so much weight, needs to be defined. What is a leader? A description of what is expected of them needs to be clearly displayed. By doing so, goals and expectations can be charted and measured with understanding. Growth and/or failure can be seen and documented.

Once leadership is defined, there are other aspects that come into view. The making of a leader is a thought. The thoughts and behaviors that these persons bring to the table, group, or organization determine how the journey is navigated. Whether it be a family, church, school, small business, or major corporation, leadership sets the environmental atmosphere. The venue or arena affects the preparation of a leader. This preparation may involve breeding in special schools, association with iconic members of society or financial status, years spent detached from family and familiarity, or years tending sheep.

A leader can be a visionary, but a visionary may not always be a leader. One can envision a futuristic goal and fantastic possibilities but not be able to light the flame of enthusiasm under his team or get anything needed to operate. Whereas another can envision a goal, strategize how to accomplish it, and stir everyone around and on all levels to get on board totally and achieve it with gratification. This can be seen in the secular world, past and present, in business and in politics. In the Bible, there are biblical examples of such happenings in leadership.

No matter what the goal or venue might be, the styles of leadership and their effects need to be examined. Leadership styles can be referred to as emotional in some cases and/or as basic. These styles have been given names such as visionary, coaching, affiliative, democratic, pacesetting, and commanding in the emotional classification. The basic styles have names such as coercive, authoritative, affiliative, democratic, pacesetter, and coach. The coercive leader does not invite the input of anyone and is fully in charge. The authoritative leader would seem to have it all together by being able to convey the mission of the organization clearly. He or she does this in such a way that they rally those around them to get on board with focused commitment. The affiliative leader is one who consistently is in touch with everyone on the team. This fosters cohesiveness and harmony in the organization. The democratic leader weighs the consensus of everyone to go forward, but this can have its drawbacks. The pacesetter leader seemingly sets high goals for themselves and everyone else. Such a leader struggles with issues and what can also be considered "head trash." Finally, the coach leader is good for developing the team for the long haul, taking the seedlings to the perfected, matured, and productive desired result.

Some have noted that no set style of leadership is perfect. What works best depends on its fit with the organization or group. Not only the fit has to be considered, but also the ability of the chosen leadership to acquiesce to change—the change of style. The need for such a change, as change in the organization occurs. Illustrations have etched that adaptation to change is a necessity if positive productivity is to happen. The need is to identify the common goal and collaborate as necessary to achieve it. Also, radical readjustment to established traditional strategies must be applied when needed. It is evident that the same thing all the time becomes archaic, or like a shoe that did fit as a child, it does not fit the same now as an adult because of growth and change in fashion, as an example.

Further examination of leadership styles proves that some are transformational, others are transactional, and there are those that are a type of laissez-faire. These differing styles may impact leadership effectiveness. Through observation and research, it has been implicated that leadership has a significant effect on an organizational body. The combination of leadership style, work environment, coupled with job satisfaction, greatly affects employee performance. Consequently, this combination affects the community and society. This would reflect the sociological aspect of leadership.

Leadership and sociology put forth aspects of human society and its behavior in groups and relationships. A major factor in this is understanding how groups operate and having the ability to work with people and do it well. The other side of this coin is to select and train leaders, anticipating the future operation of the group. The unique selection and training of these leaders should be based on the specific mechanics and dynamics of the group. The ingredients involved in understanding the group include background, trends in participation, communication relationships/relativity and cohesiveness, to name a few. The interaction of the leader greatly affects the behavior of the group.

Besides the sociological aspect and society, the sole foundation of all institutions seems to be traced back to the family. Therefore, a good place to view leadership is in its "solar plexus," the family. Within this familiar and unique unit is the biological facet. Add to this the facet of social effects on society, then the facet of placement, status, and acknowledgment based on gender. Dwelling on this is not so much the established personage of the male, but even more so that of the female. Alongside these many facets, there is the functionality of the family. Designations of reproduction responsibilities, childcare, coordination of economics, provision, finances, and initiative in the expression of love and affection are all functions of the family.

Leadership and organizational culture are another aspect of this vast subject of leadership. Organizational culture encompasses the structure that identifies an entity as an organization. It consists of the many facets that denote the significantly ingenious style that it possesses. Organizational culture can also be considered an unseen force or presence. Such a force or presence has the ability to attract and draw the desired audience and retain them. This same presence can also repel and discourage those that one desires to attract.

Retention in a group or organization often correlates with its leadership. Retention is the state of people remaining with an organization or not and the reasons why. The state of retention tends to be more strongly influenced by factors other than money. It is possible to retain persons solely on their allegiance to an entity or because of a legacy. This situation may not be the best. However, more readily through leadership, people seem to be retained when they sense someone cares about them. In addition to this factor, there is the growth and developmental factor, among other factors. Promotion of an agenda that energizes an individual and is relevant to their goals helps retention happen.

The ultimate leader in leadership is the Triune God, unequivocally. He sets His agenda, directives, outcomes, and promises not by trial and error but by His word. The sovereign and executive decisions of God are absolute, yet He hears the requests and cries of His people. He actively responds to their supplications according to His will. The leadership of Jehovah God is seen in the Old Testament. In the New Testament, one has the opportunity to observe Christ's preparation of the apostles and their subsequent leadership. The New Testament is also rich in examples of leadership and its consequences, as seen in the book called Revelation. More precisely to note are the examples found in the messages to the seven churches.

Leadership in the modern day has many platforms. On the secular platform, the motivation or choice of leadership may be generated by what works to bring in the biggest profits. In the family, established landmarks and values hold in some areas but are swayed and waived in others. These actions in the family give way to disturbing outcomes. Modern leadership in government seems to be strongly tainted by politics. Interestingly enough, in the church sector, there seems to be politics on some fronts too. Besides this, it is needful to look at Christian leadership here and now and what Christendom is doing. The leadership's response to the need and cry of our time merits examination.

Dear reader, as you travel through these pages, may you be stirred to betterment in whatever arena or venue you are in. There is much invested in us. Let us not be remiss and lose out on opportunities and guideposts that are sent our way. We have come to visit, read, and be exposed to these examples and instructions on purpose and for a reason. May we truly fulfill the purpose and assignment that the Lord has for us, ardently and without hesitation.

CHAPTER 1

Leadership Defined

A. Definition of Leadership

Leadership can be defined as the act or ability to direct or lead. This term may also be applied to a governing group of leaders—the ones shouldering the responsibility for the direction and guidance of a group, organization, or enterprise. All of these define what is determined as leadership. The definition of leadership needs to carry with it the title of leader also. Synonyms that describe this are trailblazer, forerunner, guide, author, captain, pioneer, prince, and chief, to name a few. A leader is the one who directs, has the principal role, and, conclusively, is the head.

B. Visionary versus Leader

With the image of such a person marching forward physically or on paper, the quandary to deal with is whether they are a visionary or indeed a leader. When thinking of a visionary, a definition of dreamer or one that is impractical may come to mind. This individual often sees what could be or is out of the box per se. Their vision illumes when others are usually chanting, it can't be done; it's not practical; it does not make sense; wait, not yet; and let's see, maybe later. The visionary may not have the ingenuity to bring their dream to fruition or the gifted finesse to rally the necessary individuals to sign on to the dream. A true leader, on the other hand, tends to not only have vision and foresight but also the charisma and ability to draw others into the dream and the desire to accomplish it enthusiastically. This leader proceeds to get the project completed with all needed parties contributing fully and in unison. Thus, I'm inclined to believe that not all visionaries are leaders, and some "truly good" leaders can possess the gift of being a visionary.

C. Secular Leadership

Upon thinking of secular leadership, the principles and standards that one is guided by tend to change. Although some organizations and leaders of such entities claim that they are founded on biblical principles, their actions and goals reflect otherwise. In the secular realm, the values of the world—wealth, power, prestige, and popularity—lunge foremost rather than reverence to God in all that is done. Often, it is noted that these things are acquired by any means possible and at anyone's expense, livelihood, or even life. The rewards under this form of leadership may come in the form of accommodations and material or monetary bonuses. These rewards are temporal and often times conditional based on the approval of the boss. The agreements and contracts involved here tend to have some degree of deception. The interpretation of right and wrong may be weighed according to the whim of the leader or said leadership. A great deal of manipulation may be involved here.

There are other aspects that compose worldly leadership, also known as secular leadership, meaning that it is not affiliated with religious influence. In view of these, it is necessary to keep in mind what is at the heart of business around the world. The answer to this is usually the acquisition of profits. Thus, it is needful to seek out the strategy that generates such an outcome or fuels this engine. It has been known that many businesses incorporate *Who Moved My Cheese* by Spencer Johnson as a mandatory training tool for their employees. Although this book is entertaining, it presents some very valuable lessons that can be applied to business and everyday life. Since leadership here moves with what is profitable, if one observes that their chief source is dwindling and not as productive as before, it is necessary to address the matter. Some observe, search out, and implement relative practical action that produces the desired effect. Others continue to wait and see until the situation becomes dire before implementing some undefined action, which, with "luck," renders the desired effect. Finally, there are still those who remain relentless and unwilling to change even in the face of negative productivity.

Besides noting source and productivity, other tools of business leadership involve the making of what are referred to as SMART goals and also a code of ethics. Upon looking at these other tools, it is good to explore the SMART in the goals. This exploration reveals specific (clear and exact), measurable, attainable, relevant, and time-honored goals. Good leadership tends to apply these principles in business. Besides these principles, a formulated equation known for excellent leadership is the application of John C. Maxwell's *The 21 Irrefutable Laws of Leadership*.

Maxwell addresses at the very beginning a point not actually spoken of earlier. This point is that some leadership may look promising and excellent when operating in a relatively small arena or organization but deteriorate with the increasing magnitude of the organization. It has been found that this can be readjusted. A person's leadership ability is not etched in stone. It can change for the better with effort. The laws presented by Maxwell hold such valuable instructions in many aspects. Priorities, influence, respect, reassessment, strengths, returns, reward, intuition, and timing are some of the things in the mix that make leadership. These jewels, when utilized well, make for formidable leadership.

Taking a moment to dwell on one of these jewels, I think of the power that influence has in the arena of politics. In this arena, there are repercussions that influence has had that have altered history. In current times, this generation has the privilege of witnessing the influence of Barack Obama. The aura of leadership exudes from within such a man. Here is an example to show that the attitude of leadership does not start when someone is thrust in front of people. This mindset was simmering long before the presentation. Thus, it becomes likewise evident in the person's body language and gestures.

These things seal and fortify the words then spoken by the gifted or otherwise prepared individual. This phenomenon is intensified when the individual incorporates the concerns of his audience and finds common ground that benefits all. Leanne states, "This language resonated with the audience, tapping into patriotic sentiment. In a masterful way, Obama also wove in…words and principles reached across divisions of race, class, and party, helping him connect with the audience."[1]

D. Biblical Leadership

In the biblical realm, the ultimate goal is to please God. The rewards fall under the blessings of the Lord. This realm functions with guidelines built on the foundation of the Holy Scriptures. Examples of biblical leadership have shown those who heeded Jehovah's instruction, those who were contrary and repented, and those who dwelt in total rebellion. The examples thereof reveal the consequential results, which serve as roadmaps for life for generations that follow. Those who signed on in this realm of history rarely worked with written contracts but rather with covenants between the specific chosen individual and Jehovah. The New Testament shows forth a different contract with the dedication devoted to the "Great Commission" (Matt. 28:19–20).

Moses showed up for a job that he did not think he was prepared for—a true example of stepping into a position and wondering how one landed up in the position. The main motivation in the life of this great leader had to be his ultimate belief in the great I AM (Ex. 3:14). Before delving into the different biblical leaders, the thought of God being the greatest CEO comes to mind. Such a thought seems to be exemplified in the parable of the three servants and the talents (Matt. 25:14–30). Here one may note observation of the Master, assessment, productivity, projected results, and expected returns. Here, one may

---

[1] Shel Leanne, *Say It Like Obama and Win!* (New York, New York: The McGraw Hill Companies, 2010), 16.

also note what may be considered an executive decision. This is food for thought, hmm.

However, let's embark on a journey through some biblical leaders. As aforesaid, Moses, viewed as an awesome leader, did not seem to have leadership in mind when he started out. His background prepared him for the task that Jehovah would assign. This chosen vessel of Hebrew birth, raised as Egyptian royalty with Hebrew nurturing, became a fugitive and a shepherd, which were his prerequisites for the task (Ex. 2:1–25). With a multicultural background, Moses experienced rollercoaster challenges throughout his life. Yet despite all this, he was Jehovah's chosen servant and remained faithful. He went from privileged to menial, from honored to criminally on the run, dealing with impairment and esteem issues; he was thrust from obscurity to the forefront and awesomeness. While navigating through his challenges, he communed directly with God and led an extremely large mass of people. He persevered, though, being set before rebellious royalty (the pharaoh) and a people who scrutinized, criticized, rebelled, and harbored distrust.

Despite their unfavorable behavior toward Moses, for these same people, he still had the capacity to intercede for them before the Lord. Because of the Israelites infuriating Moses, he was disciplined by God and did not enter the promised land (Exodus through Deuteronomy). He accepted this also. God blessed him to be an example of faithfulness, from the burning bush (Ex. 3:1–12) and beyond. He's an example of love and compassion, even when wronged by others—those that he will willingly turn to and intercede for. Moses showed that even though he was the one who communed directly with God, he was still humble enough to heed wise counsel. He did this with Jethro, his father-in-law, whom was not even of his own culture (Ex. 18:13–26). In a simple form, he also had succession planning in place, as seen by his interactions with Joshua (Ex. 17:10–15; 24:12–18; 32:15–19; 33:7–11; Num. 27:15–23; 34:1–2, 16–17; Deut. 1:35–38; 3:21–28; 31:1–8; 34:9–12; Josh. 1:1–9).

Another example to look at while scrutinizing biblical leadership is Esther. This champion exemplified obedience and respect to a parental figure. She trusted in the wise counsel and guidance of

Mordecai, whom "fate" (God) had put in her life. The book of Esther does not record the name(s) of God directly. She has the frightful courage to venture into unfamiliar territory and circumstances—her potential queen prep. She knew the power of fasting and seeking the favor of the Most High. This champion exhibited awakening "for such a time as this" and resolve, "If I perish, I perish" (Esth. 4:14–16).

Acknowledging God as the true CEO of biblical leadership, an example of going against the executive's plan and format is truly seen in the review of Jeroboam. Although he had clear and direct instruction from God, he chose to do anything and everything contrary to what God wanted for Israel (1 Kings 11:26 through 14:20). As in business, God communicates His desired plan for His "employees" and expected outcomes. He incorporates His judgments and rewards them accordingly. God gives us time to prove ourselves in response to His word and His calling. I often ponder why Jeroboam so blatantly chose to disobey God. Jeroboam's actions seemed to set the precedent for the succeeding kings of the ten tribes of Israel and their ultimate downfall.

The leadership of David could be described as that of an individual who signed on for the long haul. David possessed acknowledgment, love, and worship of the Almighty God from his youth and throughout his life (2 Sam. 22:1–51; 23:1–5; the Psalms). He was consistent in his sincerity, although overlooked by his father and brothers at different times and disdained by his wife Michal (2 Sam. 6:16–23). David, from his youth, put no limits on God, as seen with Goliath (1 Sam. 17:12–58). He was not above seeking God's forgiveness when he messed up (2 Sam. 12:1–25; Ps. 51). He was gracious in accepting the LORD's judgment, as with Bathsheba and also the numbering of Israel (2 Sam. 11:1–12:25; 24:1–17; 1 Chron. 21:1–17).

David had the ability to draw people to him (1 Sam. 22:1–2). This can be seen as the law of magnetism. In regards to this law, John C. Maxwell says, "Believe it or not, who you attract is not determined by what you want. It's determined by who you are."[2] Although

---

[2]   John C. Maxwell, *The 21 Irrefutable Laws of Leadership* (New York, New York: Harper Collins Leadership, 1998 and 2007), 104.

this seemed to be true of David at this time of his life, with men of a somewhat rough nature, this did not fully define his life. From such a time in his life, it is believed that he drew the character that was necessary in his many conquests. As Maxwell has expressed, a person can always change his levels and the ones that he attracts. David did this with the help and guidance of God Almighty and also with his ability to generate encouragement and motivation from within himself (2 Sam. 22). This great leader was a man after God's own heart (1 Sam. 13:14; Ps. 89:18–20). The Almighty God chose David's lineage as the earthly hereditary lineage of Jesus Christ (1 Sam. 7:8–29; 1 Sam. 16:3–13; 1 Chron. 17:7–15).

CHAPTER 2

Leadership Styles and Effects

A. The Coercive Leader

The coercive leader does not invite the input of anyone and is fully in charge. For the most part, this would truly seem like a dictatorship, whether in global politics or business. The wisdom of Solomon advises against this and says, "Where no counsel is, the people fall: but in the multitude of counsellors there is safety" (Prov. 11:14). Another phase of this style of leadership causes one to think of an authoritative figure who is privy to someone's indiscretions and uses that to manipulate and compel. This manipulative behavior fosters the leader's selfish means and acquisitions. Coerce speaks of compulsion, intimidation, having no regard for individuals, dominance, and bringing about things with force. This functioning may seem to thrive for a time, but biblical truths do come to pass in this life. Thus, at some point, sooner or later, the just returns will come. It is said, "Whatsoever a man soweth, that shall he also reap" (Gal. 6:7–9). For those who are inclined to think that their crafty deeds are not noted, there is a rude awakening according to Malachi the prophet (Mal. 3:14–18).

Under such a regime, followers, employees, or constituents are not likely to remain because of dedication or allegiance. With such tyrannical leadership, the recipients will more than likely remain because of fear and/or desperation, feeling that they may have no other recourse. This generates an atmosphere of oppression and dissatisfaction, coupled with never-ending weariness. In this arena, things are accomplished, but the accomplishments seem to be empty victories or conquests. Ideally, the coercive leader is not the leader of preference.

B. The Authoritative Leader

The authoritative leader would seem to have it all together. They have the ability to convey the mission of the organization clearly. This individual does this in such a way that they rally those around them to get on board with their focused commitment. A favorable combo this seems to be, but valued input may possibly not be included in the picture. If input is heard, it could be lightly received and not truly incorporated. The facade of having it altogether may not hold in this instance if a solid foundation with irrefutable laws and gifts is not in place. Conclusively, the viability of the organization under this leadership requires more than an authoritative leader if it is to have longevity and thrive.

C. The Affiliative Leader

This leader is one who consistently stays in touch with everyone on the team. Such action tends to foster cohesiveness and harmony in an organization. Depending on the size of the organization, this has the potential to cause severe wear on the leader. With wear, one anticipates the predisposition of diminished functioning at optimal levels physically for this leader. This also means a possibly shortened life span in the organization or literally in life. The positive part of this is that the recipients have a bond with their leader and, very likely, with each other. People are moved when you know them by name and have a healthy relationship with them. This builds the recipient's self-esteem, and that is a very good thing. The interaction that exists here affords the leader the opportunity to observe each team member, their productivity, and, even more crucially, their integrity. This is the heart of the matter that will determine the image and reputation of the organization.

Moreover, the precedent for this has already been etched in the Holy Scriptures. God shows us that we are individualized and valued. The hairs on our head are numbered, and we are much more than the value of many sparrows (Matt. 10:29–31). Jesus took time and spent it with Zacchaeus and his family (Luke 19:1–10). Even with the disciples, Jesus was not only preaching and teaching the written word. He knew their lives involved more than bare ministry, as when He took time to heal Peter's mother-in-law (Matt. 8:14–15). Taking a glance back, one may note that Jesus's initial visitation to the places of the disciples' occupations and His dialogue with them got them on board with His earthly ministry (Matt. 4:18–22). Thus, the affiliative style offers a positive blueprint for how to conduct and grow business and ministry.

D. The Democratic Leader

The democratic leader weighs the consensus of everyone to go forward. This type of action and leadership can, and most assuredly does, have its drawbacks. In this style, even if the leader is a visionary, not much can be achieved because of varied opinions, attitudes, and "I want it my way, or else." The democratic style tends to weaken the unified strength of the organization. Possibly a seemingly good example of this disparity and effect may be seen in the book of 1 Corinthians of the biblical Scriptures. Here Paul swiftly addresses the divisions among the brethren (1 Cor. 1:11–13). In the same manner, if there are too many differences and votes in opposite directions, progress is stalled, and one ends up going nowhere.

The good part about this style is that it has a platform where those involved can voice their thoughts. Thus, the leader here can get an idea or assessment of the quality, education, intellectual abilities, capabilities, and potentials of those in the group, organization, or ministry. Though there is a positive facet to this style of leadership, something still seems to be missing the mark. The major component that seems to be missing is the fact that the leader is to be the one who guides the group to the chosen destination. This does not seem to be done well by throwing up a bunch of votes and waiting to see which lands on top or whose voice is the loudest. This was not the case when Moses was leading the children of Israel (Ex. 33:1, 12–17). Neither was this the case with Joshua when he addressed Israel about their two opinions (Josh. 24:15–22). Even though democracy in the democratic style has its moments, there is a need for affirmative action—the need for the true leader to shine forth before the people. In order that the group may go forth in unity and not be contaminated with disgruntled constituents whose votes were not reflected in the final decision. In the long run, someone has to be deemed chiefly responsible for the decisions that are made. Decisions for strategies, blueprint plans and programs, measurable achievement, timelines, starts, and finishes—these all need a true and significant leader.

E. The Pacesetter Leader

The pacesetter leader seemingly sets high goals for themselves and everyone else. They struggle within with issues that can be considered "head trash." Head trash can be progressively crippling. It has the ability to taint one's behavior. If it is not dealt with, it can eventually be detrimental, explosive, and damaging emotionally, mentally, and possibly physically. Elements of head trash are fear, arrogance, insecurity, control, anger, guilt, and paranoia. In the pacesetter style of leadership, the goals may be attained for a while, but the negativity flows down from the leader through the organization, group, etc. This negativity resulting from whatever head trash exists has to be acknowledged and willingly changed if the organization is to have true success. Squillaro and Thomas have stressed the importance of addressing head trash:

> Fear, arrogance, insecurity, control, anger, guilt, and paranoia—these "demons" can derail even the most promising leaders…when leaders' Head Trash goes unaddressed, it can have a profoundly negative impact on them, their teams,

> and their whole businesses... The ash heap...is piled high with victims of Head Trash: leaders who've failed to recognize their shortcomings until it was too late; followers who were too traumatized to care; and businesses that lost talent and profits...when you recognize you have a form of Head Trash, and are willing to do the work to overcome it, you can be an exemplary leader. [3]

F. The Coach Leader

The coach style is good for developing the team for the long haul. This leader takes the team members from their seedling state all the way through. The coach type follows through with the team members to get them to the perfect, mature, and productive desired result. This leadership style is comforting and reassuring. In this style, it is believed that the coach has the ability to identify potential and develop it. Also, with this development he nurtures and knows when to release control, giving way to creativity, expansion, and positive outcomes. Such guidance seems applicable in the arena of business as well as that of Christendom.

However, in Christendom, this style leans toward noting some qualities and actions of what is deemed the five-fold ministry (Eph. 4:11–12). Here the prophet or prophetical person sees, notes, or identifies the gifting that will come forth in and through the individual. The pastor nurtures and speaks life over his "flock," the subjects' lives. While the pastor does this, he keeps a watchful eye on the development, giving it space to stretch out and drawing in when needed. In tandem, the teacher instructs so that the seedlings will be fully knowledgeable and equipped as they mature, and their roots will have stability. Thus, the coach style is beneficial to the body and to the organization. It has been researched and noted by Goleman, et al. that no set style is perfect; it depends on its fit with the organiza-

---

[3] Tish Squillaro, Timothy I. Thomas, *Head Trash* (Austin: Emerald Book Company, 2013), 127

tion. Not only the fit has to be considered, but also the ability of the chosen leadership to acquiesce to changes in style as they occur in the organization, group, family, etc.

CHAPTER 3

Various Aspects

A. The Sociological Approach

Let's take a look at leadership in the light of sociology. The cultural and environmental factors of human society—these factors concerning its development, operation, and functioning—basically define sociology. In other words, sociology can be considered the scientific study of society. This study specifically handles group behavior and all kinds of human relationships. Based on such a premise, it becomes necessary to view sociological relevance with reference to the family, community organizations, and government. To this list, it is imperative to also add communication and distribution, consumption and distribution of goods, race and radicalism, and finally, relations for a finer, or as it is called, richer living. Thus, in such a study, we comprehend the sociological influence on leadership in our lives.

The family would seem to be the solar plexus of society. Why this thought, one may wonder. It is because the family is at the very center and heart of society. If the family is hit with a "gut" punch, it affects and radiates throughout the entire being of the social system or body. The family core in this current day and time appears to be boldly going through phases. Society has incorporated altered variations of the formerly accepted traditional family unit. Thus, the biological equation, teaching, and reproductive channels have taken shifts, some generally accepted, some refused, and some indecisive.

As one views the shifts in family units, it sometimes seems like the pendulum of society is swinging—swinging from the standards of biblical principles to the extremes of depraved ungodly behavior.

With these shifts, the authority of leadership in the family seems to have disseminated from the parents to the children and the general media in some cultures. As a result, widespread lawlessness seems to have proliferated in day-to-day life. Lack of respect and reverence for the elderly is also prevalent and rampant. However, in the midst of all this, there is still a remnant of those who hold proven and traditional values dear. Those who comply with the instructions given to the children of Israel in the book of Deuteronomy (Deut. 6:6,7) do reap the benefits thereof. These benefits are not confined to the Jewish culture only but can be seen in the families that teach their children valued principles consistently.

In efforts to curtail the out-of-order disruptive behavior, the family and society turn to government and politics. It has been seen that when parents can no longer control their children, they turn to others for help. These others are the authorities, governing bodies, politicians, and social systems that provide help. Some of these others move disruptive children from dysfunctional family units to group homes. These others may involve the police, social workers, lawyers, judges, and counselors. The group homes may indeed make situations worse and produce hardened individuals for the future of society. With these adjustments, leadership is no longer initiated in the home but stems from the hands and offices of the group home employees, textbooks, lawyers, political officials, etc.

Although what's spoken of here seems to involve a small percentage of the general population, this eventually affects all of us. The effects are noted in prejudices against business, laws and legislation that advance one set and restrict another, and prosperity and poverty disparity among varied cultures and classes. One finds that the governing decisions appear to favor the concerns of the ones making them rather than the ones that have the greatest need. Such leadership reflects a lack of sensitivity and compassion. Objectivity and integrity are also missing in this package.

On a positive note, in the sociological aspect, these situations encourage community constituents to rise as leaders with enthusiasm to serve their surroundings. I've seen civic associations initiated by concerned neighbors. Thriving and productive associations existing for decades and addressing the needs and concerns of the community were observed. However, some associations are no longer in existence, while others are still operating and effective. From an external view of leadership, it seems that those being served were not motivated to buy into the necessary mechanics of operation in some cases. Consequently, in such a community, once the active operators moved or aged out, the operations and association ceased. In contrast, the association that may have been inclusive of all parties taking an active part in operations had a notedly different outcome. The inclusive association incorporated meetings for sharing information to make members aware. This community effort sparked desire in its younger constituents. Thus, there were younger members willing and ready to take and receive the baton of operations when the time for the older officers came.

The ones who assumed the responsibility of the inclusive association were interested and involved from the very beginning of their leadership. They appeared to broaden the awareness of the community in the sight of local politicians to acquire waiting and available benefits for constituents. These leaders proved their diligence during an immediate community disaster. They checked on neighbors by calling and even going door to door. This team readily kept neighbors aware of access to help before, during, and after. Even with the mayor's office, the comptroller, commissioners of DEP (Department of Environmental Protection) and Emergency Operations, television news networks, etc. involved, this team remained approachable, responsive, and caring. These exhibited leadership qualities breed confidence in the recipients thereof. The behavior of this team strongly implicates that they possess a very essential foundational brick, known as ethics. Not only possessing ethics but putting them into practice. Nelson and Economy speak about this feature as follows:

> *Ethics* are standards of beliefs and values that guide conduct, behavior, and activities. Ethics provide boundaries for our actions and help us do the right thing-not just talking about doing the right thing, but really doing it…some or all of the following personal qualities constitute ethical behavior:
>
> - Honesty
> - Integrity
> - Impartiality
> - Fairness
> - Loyalty
> - Dedication
> - Responsibility
> - Accountability
>
> Remember: When you set an example as an ethical leader…and encourage others to adopt them.[4]

Leadership examples in the community were very evident. The results of such efforts offer lessons to be learned by society.

Moving from family and community, one comes to the visitation of the sociological aspect of leadership in government and business. This visitation enters a much larger sphere, which is filled with multiple diversities. The ultimate goal here is to find the happy medium where desired outcomes are accomplished and everyone is served and satisfied. This, at times, seems only possible in a "perfect world" or utopia. The leader in this sphere must strive to successfully

---

[4] Bob Nelson, Peter Economy, *The Management Bible* (Hoboken: John Wiley & Sons Inc., 2005), 268

deal with diversities in race, nationalities, sexuality, party affiliations, and cultures. They must be knowledgeable in knowing how people operate and, therefore, how people respond to certain stimuli. Consequently, with these tools, one can project calculated outcomes and responses. A well-adjusted leader has the ability to manage these relationships.

B. The Family Unit

In continuing to look at the various aspects of leadership, one looks more intently at the family unit. For this present mild study, the chosen subjects are found in the biblical accounts of families and their presentations of leadership. At this juncture, a look at Abraham seems feasible. The leadership account of this patriarch is unique. He has no model or leader to glean from. There was no guidebook or procedure manual to refer to as he journeyed through this new venture. Contrary to the children of Israel, whose parents were instructed to rehearse their guidance to them consistently (Deut. 6:7–9), this was not for Abraham. He was not to follow or rely on the customs of Terah, his father, an idolater. This patriarch was moving out on a bare slate with only his faith in the Lord (Gen. 12:1–5; Heb. 11:8–10). His whole future was based on his directives and relationship with Jehovah and Abraham's unconditional obedience to the Almighty God (Gen.15:6, 13, 14). As the head of his family, once he received his instructions from God, he moved away without hesitation, taking his immediate family with him and Lot, his fatherless nephew. In his position as a leader, he guided those following him to the desired goal and aim.

Abraham, as a leader, exhibited impartiality, integrity, and compassion in his dealings with Lot (Gen. 13, 14, and 18). Even though Lot did not deal honorably with his uncle, it did not taint his uncle's actions toward him (Gen. 18:19). His Uncle Abraham was the true patriarch. In the same way that a father, leader, or advocate would intercede for a dear one, Abraham dialogued with the Lord on behalf of Lot. A thought as Christ also interceded for us before the Father (John 17). Also, while thinking on Abraham, I was led to muse on how this man presented himself. Knowing that he would be the model blueprint to set the precedence for his descendants, he was diligent to the best of his ability (Gen. 15:1, 5; 17:1–8; 2 Chron. 20:7; Prov. 13:22; Isa. 41:8; Jas. 2:23).

The humanness of this forefather evidenced itself in his harkening to his wife, Sarah's counsel, which was contrary to the plan of Jehovah. However, Abraham rectified the matter and aligned with the plan of God, which yielded blessings for him and his descendants to come. This father's ultimate test of obedience was the impending sacrifice of Isaac. As a leader in his family, this time was not up for discussion or consultation with his wife. Yet it is interesting to note from the dialogue of Isaac with his father, evidence is here that Abraham trained his son diligently in his established customs of worship and honor to God (Gen. 22:1–18). This champion is an example of what an initial leader should be: an example of setting the footprints for others to follow while having mistakes and challenges, nevertheless, persevering no matter what and accomplishing one's goal.

Another example that comes to mind in the subject of leadership and the family is the parable of the prodigal son (Luk.15:11–32). Here, a wrench seems to be thrown into a fairly stable family existence when the younger son demands his inheritance prematurely, as it seems. The father here promotes the ability to respond, hear the request and plea, and act sensibly. As a leader, it is most important to not react with erratic and uncontrolled reactionary behavior when the unexpected comes. It is needful in leadership to truly hear and tune in to the voices and needs of one's subordinates. Such character and sensitivity are important at home, at the office, in business, and in organizations, as well as at church. Even Christ was in tune with his disciples' voicing of inadequacy during His ministry and responded (Mk. 6:31–44; 8:1–9; 9:14–29; Lk. 9:12–17).

Besides heeding his son's request, the father of the prodigal exemplifies compassion, mercy, and restoration. He also exercises his right to make an executive decision when his son returns, despite what each of the sons thought should be executed. Similarly, despite the chatter of family members and others about what's fair and what's not, ideally the parent has the prerogative to decide and to judge according to their own convictions. So also, God has the power to forgive, restore, and reconcile us. Personally speaking, I reflect back on times of childhood, remembering when a sibling might express, "that's not fair." In times like these, it was evident that my parents knew the hearts of their children—knew when one was repentant and when one just wanted the gratification of seeing punishment given. This execution of leadership is responsible for setting the policies that one will live by. The grace and mercy granted will hopefully put a demand on one's ability and initiative to do better going forward.

As one continues to view the family unit in this subject, there are some that are thrust into leadership without formal authority in some sort of way. An example of this that comes to mind is the account of Naomi and Ruth (Ruth 1–4). In an era and culture where the males of a family were considered the head of the household, Naomi and Ruth were stripped of such a position. They were both stripped of their domestic coverage, benefits, distinction, comfort, and providers. These terms or states of being came into play as the result of the unexpected and seemingly untimely deaths of their husbands (Ruth 1:1–5). For Ruth, it was the loss of her husband. However, with an even greater impact, Naomi suffered the loss of her husband and both of her sons. The traditional family structure here has been totally redesigned involuntarily. Naomi is not a male but has to assume the leadership of this unconventional family unit. Here, no ceremonial bestowment is spoken of. The only herald here is that of the cares of life and the desperation to make things work and survive. This is very relevant for our daily lives, even in these current times.

In this leadership example, one sees not so much hierarchy but collaboration, mentoring, and commitment. Ruth and Naomi are locked into each other for the common good. The very memorable verse of this book, "And Ruth said, Intreat me not to leave thee…for whither thou goest, I will go" (Ruth 1:16), speaks the essence of commitment. A commitment like this is needed for accomplishment and success on all levels—in family and in business. It is needed equally for the mentor as well as the mentee, peer to peer, family members, and coworkers alike. Locking into the goal here yielded such surmountable benefits and blessings for Naomi and Ruth. In addition, it blessed many others, such as Boaz, and generations to come.

Naomi poured into her daughter-in-law what she knew, and the Lord truly guided her. Ruth, with what she received and was accepted for, had nothing but love and devotion for this woman of God. This young woman, in turn, felt comfortable sharing her experiences with her mother-in-law. They both mutually grew in wisdom, character, and so much more. Ferrazzi says, "It's the commitment to the shared mission and to each other—to ensure each other's success, to have each other's backs, to coach each other, and to help each other grow and develop. That's the way forward."[5] This book displays how the disposition and development of one can be readjusted with changes in life and events. A prime example of this is the contrast between Naomi at the beginning of this epic (Ruth 1:19–21) and her at the end (Ruth 4:3–17).

C. Organizational Culture

The aspect of organizational culture is awesome. This invisible entity must be acknowledged by leadership and managed. Organizational culture can be perceived as the social and psychological atmosphere of one's organization, brought about by the input of values and behaviors. This invisible presence, which is formidable and in true attendance, possesses expectations and experiences of the said organization. It also holds not only values but also philosophy. Much of this is seen in the self-image and internal operations. Recognition of such a culture is also noted in the way that the organization interacts externally with the outside world and its projected expectations. This aspect includes and enfolds the foundational bricks of beliefs, customs, and similar attitudes. The attitudes here are known to be shared and common. Characteristics of this presence are seen in the development of rules, both written and unwritten, that have evolved

---

[5] Keith Ferrazzi, *Leading Without Authority* (New York: Currency, 2020), 126

over time and are held as valid. Organizational culture may also be referred to as corporate culture.

One may believe that leadership establishes and influences this culture more if the leader is in charge from the inception of the organization. However, if such a culture has had the opportunity to take root prior to current leadership, it very well may be business as usual or a grave upset in operations. With business as usual, leadership succumbs and is compliant with the culture. The upset might come in the event of a leader or leadership attempting to sway the behavior of the organization in another or new direction. This can be a blend or a pull and tug; either way, there are far-reaching returns.

The far-reaching returns are evidenced in the manner in which the organization transacts business. Moreover, the treatment and care of members, employees, and even customers have an effect. Consequently, the community, whether local or global, is impacted. In addition, an atmosphere that would nurture the allowance of decision-making, development, and offering new ideas is also influenced. The granting of freedom to have personal expression may likely be affected. This culture shows up in the way that power, communication, and information stream through the channels of hierarchy. The cumulative dedication and commitment to collective goals and objectives and the measurement thereof from the team or employees are impressed by this.

This invisible prominent entity is such a powerful force. It has a major hand in setting the precedence for the productivity and performance of the organization. It sets the guidelines for the care and service of customers. The issuance of protocols governing product quality, safety, and environmental concerns is formulated and influenced. Attendance and punctuality are likewise influenced. This influence delves into production methods, the practices of advertising and marketing, and even the creativity of new product output. Organizational culture has been found to be unique in each organization. However, it has also been found to be among the hardest things to change.

It is necessary to note that there is a shadowing twin to organizational culture, which is referred to as organizational climate. The culture and the climate, in relevance to each other, would align with analogies of coins, elements, and the sun and moon. In the analogy of coins, the culture is considered the face of the coin, and the climate is considered the flip side of the coin. In the analogy of the elements, culture is perceived as the season and climate as the daily forecast. Finally, for the sun and moon, culture is considered the sun, while climate is deemed the moon. Some have collectively surmised that culture is basically the ideologies, norms, and values that manifest themselves in stories and symbols. Understandable facts and the origination of these tend to be found and associated with the accounts of the organization's founding. For an understanding of climate, one must perceive it as being the psychological portion of an organization, which evidences itself in perceptions combined with attitudes. The implication here is that culture and climate are not the same but are strongly associated with each other.

One is inclined to believe, therefore, that culture is the greater of the two since it is based on the foundational articles of the organization. Climate, however, sets the atmosphere and how one feels, and therefore functions daily. Culture is believed to influence the climate. The culture of an organization is more enduring in the same way that the foundation of a building is established. The building may be renovated and updated, but rarely are the beams and pillars of the foundation uprooted with each renovation or enhancement. Likewise, the climate may change based on the current employees and how they feel about where they are and how they are treated. One could summarize that in an organization, the culture affirms what the organization is all about. Nevertheless, the climate is what one will sense once they have entered the door or have gone on board.

Further examination of this subject reveals that there are different types of organizational culture and climate. Some have clarified that culture has four types. The types are namely clan, adhocracy, market-oriented, and hierarchically-oriented. Clan culture is characteristic of employees functioning as an extended family within which they participate, mentor, and nurture. In adhocracy, one finds that the employees are dynamic. These are people who are not hesitant to take risks and are innovative. The market-oriented group is mainly guided by results. Their dedicated attention is to the job, involving competition and what can be measured by achievements. The fourth type of culture is the hierarchically-oriented type. Here, the employees are put through rigid protocols. The structure of the protocols involves former rules, controls, and policies. They are expected to be consistent, stable, and uniform in their functioning.

On the other hand, there are likewise four different types of organizational climate. The four types of climate are differentiated as people-oriented, rule-oriented, innovation-oriented, and goal-oriented. A people-oriented climate is mainly individual-focused. It is centered on the perceptions of the organization's workers. The rule-oriented type is rooted in the mix of policies, procedures, and rules that have been established aforetime. The climate that provides an atmosphere for creativity and innovative ways of getting the job done is referred to as an innovation-oriented climate. An organization that is focused mainly on achieving its goals is classified as possessing a goal-oriented climate.

No one type of culture is noted right for all organizations. It is necessary to find the one that is suited as the right fit for one's precise organization. This needs to be considered in the same way that not every leadership style is suitable for every organization. It has been determined that, of organizational culture and climate, culture has been deemed the more formidable of the two. The culture, though it may be strong, can be changed. Such transformation is possible with the guidance of a very important component, leadership. The right leadership can change the culture. An essential action for any leader, especially a new one, is to assess and understand an organization's culture. After this action, it is necessary to determine whether change is required or needful.

In addition to what has been mentioned, there is yet another part concerning culture in the behavior of an organization. That part is thought of and referenced as spirituality. Contrary to one's initial thought, this has nothing to do with religion, theological study, or God. Spirituality that happens in the workplace or organization is the viable existence of people that is strengthened, which in turn is strengthened through productive work that is meaningful. This spirituality possesses a spiritual sense of community, connection, and involvement. The understanding of spirituality in the workplace pulls from ethics, leadership, motivation, and values. To this combination must be added the balance of life and work. Organizations that enfold spirituality may be referred to as spiritual organizations. Concerning the characteristics of a spiritual organization, Robbins says, "Spiritual organizations are concerned with helping people develop and reach their full potential...Strong sense of purpose... Focus on individual development...Trust and openness...Employee empowerment...Toleration of employee expression...They allow people to be themselves."[6]

D. Retention

Retention can be surmised as the state of people remaining with an organization or not and the reason why. Most assuredly, in either case, it is needful to examine the players (people) involved. Some have concluded that there are far greater issues than finances, which are to motivate, stir, and nurture faithfulness to an organization and its leadership. Many stress that beyond the money issue is the need to know that those who are in charge of them sincerely care about them and their needs. In the mix is the allowable place for growth and development. People have the need to know or be nestled in a culture that supports and respects them. The organization should preferably foster a healthy balance between life and work and promote positive relationships. To the discriminating individual, retention is more bent on quality and performance than just the numerical growth of the organization.

Proactive leadership aids in the matter of retention. Leaders who are genuinely aware of the needs of their charges can be proactive. They have the opportunity to anticipate, plan, and be prepared for changes and circumstances. A coaching-type leadership style might be one that promotes retention intently. Atmospheres of proactivity,

---

6   Stephen P. Robbins, *Essentials of Organizational Behavior* (Upper Saddle River: Pearson Prentice Hall, 2005), 243-244

nurturing, and motivation energize people. Such things empower individuals to reach their highest level of potential and achieve their goals. This is the soil of leadership that brings forth positive retention. On the other hand, therefore, one is inclined to believe that the absence of these key ingredients breeds negative retention, which is evidenced as exiting.

However, efforts to improve retention depend grossly on methodical changes in operation—changes in the practices of the organization alongside changes in attitudes. Subsequently, to this combination, there is the addition of a change in behavior. The stimulus or driving force of such change flows from the results of having taken a clear, true, and meaningful look at the way an organization or institution even serves its clients, members, employees, and/or recipients. For retention to be favorable, it would seem that feedback and evaluation are necessary.

One must believe that the success of retention is based on an ongoing assessment of the organization and leadership. Noting how both measure up with what they desire to do serves as a guideline to determine if they have accomplished their goals. Basically, note what works and what does not work for the ones that both are serving. The assessment of retention should be approached with the thought of becoming the best or as good as possible. This assessment should not be taken on with the attitude of only investigating to see what went wrong at the present time. Ardent effort needs to be given to ensure that retention assessment is not a one-time happening. The information gathered ought to trigger action and also the administration of rewards.

Examination of attrition and verifying the areas of its scope and magnitude are involved in the process. Recognition of where things are functioning well has to be included. In the same manner, the less-than-desired areas of functioning need to be verified. Leadership has the responsibility here to direct the necessary action for change. Once the alterations have been instituted, it will hopefully be pleasurable to see their results. At any rate, it is mandatory or needful to determine their effectiveness and document the cause and effect.

Although one may be dealing with the treatment of retention, there is a natural element here no matter how well things are formulated, and that is change itself. No matter how perfect an infant might be at birth, they change. Thus, the child, parent, family, and surrounding community must adjust to the change or dwell in constant conflict. Supply and demand may change, or the current tumultuous changes of the pandemic that rapidly ushered into being uninvitedly happened. Some change or changes, although unwarranted, may catapult the current players into a whole new arena of operation. An aid to retention is being able to adapt to change. The enhancement of this aid comes when those involved blend their efforts. The transition here becomes easier and more effective. No matter the change or changes, certain constants, such as integrity and quality, encourage loyalty and, therefore, positive retention.

Many believe and are in agreement that, in the area of retention, the recipients of decisions need to be involved in the decision-making process. It is considered that such involvement is crucial for success in retention. No matter what approach leadership chooses to take, it is paramount that the retention effort be initiated. Above all, do something, and do not stay dormant. Widely communicate the effort, gain support, and intricately get others on board. Others in precise positions aid in bringing the goals to fruition. Assess the improvement while keeping the established goals in mind. It is helpful to keep in mind that positive relationships formed with those that represent the organization and those targeted for retention are important. These positive relationships strengthen and prove to be successful for the effort.

CHAPTER 4

The Ultimate Leader— The Triune God

A. The Executive Leadership of Jehovah

So many thoughts come to mind on how to enter this segment of study. The Supreme God, who is the creator of all mankind, has no racial prejudices. This is known because mankind is something God chose to make in His own image (Gen. 1:26–27). He is neither erratic nor a demagogue, but His word and promises are firm and true (2 Cor. 1:20–21). He has proven Himself that He is not a liar and has no reason to be so (Num. 23:19). He is consistent with unshakeable stability and remains so (Psa. 90:1–2). God's judgments are true, and yet He has compassion (Gen. 4:7; Psa. 103:6–17; Rev. 19:1–5). It is good to view the leadership of Jehovah in light of the definition of leadership. The definition chosen implies that a leader is one who is a guide that leads along or goes before, leading via instruction or counsel. Some prime examples that seem to speak of this are referenced to Abram becoming Abraham, Moses and the exodus out of Egypt, and Gideon.

With Abraham, it would seem that Jehovah gave him a green light—whole access—based on his unreserved obedience. This man, who was not even raised to know or acknowledge Jehovah God in his life, having been approached by God, responded in complete and absolute obedience. As instructed and directed by Jehovah to pick up and leave his family and all that was familiar, Abraham acted in full faith (Gen. 12: 1–5; Josh. 24:2; Heb. 11:8–9). There is no blueprint, proposal, or resume submitted for this leadership. However, Scripture tells us that before we were formed, we were known (Jer. 1:5). At this juncture, a weary thought raised its head. It may seem abstract for what is being dealt with here, but it is part of this important conversation. For the individual, one may wonder if it is choice or predestination. This can be just thought of as a sprinkle of spice to think about as we navigate through life. Let us continue with Abraham being guided by an entity not seen, yet one of immeasurable magnitude. With Jehovah, He has no need to give account to anyone, yet He chooses to commune with us and respond to us.

One might ponder why it was Abraham (Abram) and not Haran or Nahor. After all, they were the sons of Terah likewise (Gen. 11:27). It may be considered because Abraham's longing desire to commune and visit with God possibly moved the heart of Jehovah (Gen. 13:3–4, 15:1–18, 17:1–13; Isa. 41:8; Gal. 3:6–9). The choosing of this patriarch rather than his brethren might be relevant to the parables of the servants (Matt. 25:14–29; Lk. 12:42–48). It is said, "For unto whomsoever much is given, of him shall be much required: and to whom men have committed much, of him they will ask the more" (Lk. 12:48b). This man would yield a much greater return in his productivity. His faithfulness projected his likelihood of achieving the spoken goal.

God blessed, corrected, instructed, and tested Abraham, yet He was approachable. Jehovah blessed His friend with wealth and to be a father of many nations (Gen.12:1–3, 15:1–15, 17:1–8, 22:15–18). He corrected him concerning Hagar and Ishmael (Gen. 21:9–14). He instructed him on the covenant and circumcision (Gen. 17:6–14). Jehovah tested Abraham with Isaac (Gen. 22:1–14). Nevertheless, God was patiently tolerant when Abraham interceded on behalf of Lot and Sodom and Gomorrah (Gen. 18:23–33). As a leader would, the Lord identified qualities in Abraham. The qualities of a father whose desire would be to leave a good and lasting inheritance for his children and descendants (Gen. 18:18–19; Prov. 13:22; Heb. 7:1–10). He noted in this patriarch one who is not tempted by wealth or monetary increase (Gen. 14:21–23). Jehovah knew that this was the one for the lineage of His Son in the plan of salvation (Gen. 3:15; Matt. 1:1–17; Lk. 1:46–55, 1:67–73; Gal. 3:14–19, 3:26–29).

Abraham proved to be a willing subject and vessel in collaboration, or more so, in partnership, with the Almighty in His divine plan. Cornwall writes, "To be God's agent is quite another matter. This we are only as we learn God's will, respond to His call, work faithfully together with Him, and find our own highest ends in fulfilling His."[7] Thus, as with Abraham, when one wholly releases themselves to God, they exceed boundaries unimaginable. This is such a blessing. It is lovely to close this notation on such a high note. However, as an afterthought, one considered the power of inheritance, whether good or bad. In these current times, it is pondered if, in some prominent families, the tragic history of untimely demises of members is due to the actions of certain ancestors. Actions that may have been ruthless, unscrupulous, and treacherous. These true dramas of life cause one to stop and take inventory of their actions daily. Therefore, one consistently strives to be more mindful of the repercussions that their actions may possess.

In all that has been spoken about Abraham, it is interesting to note that he had none of what one would esteem as formal training. He had no accredited instructor. No formal Bible college was in his credits. Yet it seemed that without a classroom or orientation session, he was trained mainly through his obedience and desire to call on the name of the Lord (Gen. 13:3, 4, 15:1, 6). Abraham, through his training, was groomed and merited an audience and communion with Melchizedek (Gen. 14:18–20). If this were a business forum, this would be among the highest awards or rewards that an employee could ever receive. This Melchizedek, a typology of Christ, the king-priest, the one with royal authority, the priest of El Elyon, the merit to have an audience with such a One is beyond measure. Within this light study, one sees the awesome guidance of God. The benefit of obedience and reward, which can be deemed as positive reinforce-

---

[7] Judson Cornwall, *Leaders: Eat What You Serve* (Shippensburg: Destiny Image Publishers, 1988), 96

ment. The spiritual and steadfast growth of Abraham, the subject, through his experiences and interaction with the Lord has been seen. And yet with all this and knowing God as Jehovah-Jireh, *The Lord will provide* (Gen. 22:8–14), and as the Almighty God, *El Shaddai* (Gen. 17:1), God affirmed to Moses another greatness. The Lord affirmed to Moses that neither Abraham, Isaac, nor Jacob had the intimacy of knowing Him as JEHOVAH, the I AM THAT I AM (Ex. 3:13–14, 6:2–3).

As one moves on to observe Jehovah's leadership in light of Moses, there are many facets to attempt to comprehend. Contrary to Abraham, Moses's visible earthly inception in the divine plan of God began at his birth. Jehovah had Moses as an exemplary figure, portraying a categorical resemblance to Christ. Moses overall fills many slots in the divine job description. He is perceived as a deliverer, an intercessor, a leader/king, a faithful servant, and a prophet. God orchestrated Moses's life in such a way that he would obtain these credentials, be able to function in these many positions, and function well in spite of himself.

This chosen vessel, born at a time when the decree of the Egyptian king was to kill the Hebrew males immediately at birth, prompted his mother to concoct a plan. This plan not only saved his life but also placed him in Pharaoh's household, where he learned Egyptian ways and culture. Yet while this was in place, because of the mechanics of this plan, his actual mother nursed him and fed him the rudiments of his Hebrew heritage. The irony of this is that his mother received wages from Pharaoh's daughter for nursing her own child (Ex. 2:1–10). Because of a series of events, Moses is rejected by the Hebrews, has to flee for safety, and is embraced by the Gentiles (Ex. 2:11–25). One can note that as a result of these happenings, this servant has received the required indoctrination lessons, the prerequisite needed prior to his call at the burning bush (Ex. 3:1–22). God, as a leader, equips us with what is needed and considers our fears and weaknesses, as He did with Moses. He added to him the empowered rod and Aaron (Ex. 4:1, 7:13).

As part of leadership, it is necessary to hold people accountable. One would believe that God did this with Moses concerning the incident of the rock and the waters of Meribah (Num. 20: 2–13). There are spiritual connotations about the rock and the water in the journey of the Israelites from Egypt. The circumstance recorded earlier in Exodus (Ex. 17:5–7) yielded a different message than the incident recorded in Numbers. For the rock in Exodus at Horeb, Moses completely followed instructions. At Meribah, he strayed from his given directives, yet still the congregation received what was intended, but his actions were counted as disobedience, with punishment rewarded. His denial of entering the promised land was his sentence. To many, this might seem very harsh and rough after all that he went through. However, one should keep in mind that the rock that Moses should have spoken to was a typology of Christ.

This typology had already been struck at Horeb, for water is a type of grace that flows. Therefore, there was no further need for "Christ" to be stricken so that water (grace) might be freely given. Just a mere spoken request was all that was needed, and this was not done by God's chosen vessel. Nevertheless, Moses clearly understood, acknowledged, and was accountable. At Meribah, Jehovah was not accepting the blame game from Moses or the fact that he was overwhelmed by the people. This servant had to simply own his actions and go forward in submission to the consequences. In *The Oz Principle*, it is said, "A thin line separates success from failure…Below that line lies excuse making, blaming others, confusion, and an attitude of helplessness…while above that line…sense of reality, ownership, commitment, solutions to problems, and determined action."[8] These values above the line are the stepping stones to accountability. Moreover, as one observes the guidance of Jehovah, there is an ascription that He draws one into accountability.

Although Moses had the noted hiccup, one believes that his ultimate guiding device was in his times of dialogue with God. These audiences with God created a tremendous bond between the Almighty and His servant, Moses. Jehovah, because of the relationship He had fostered with Moses, could be moved in His decisions

---

[8] Roger Connors, Tom Smith, and Craig Hickman, *The Oz Principle* (New York: Penguin Group, 2004), 10

(Ex. 32: 11–14; Deut. 9:1–29). Even though Moses was disciplined because of Meribah, the tender mercies of God still rewarded His faithful servant. This sets an example for leadership. The leader needs to know the heart of their follower and also show compassion and forgiveness. This should be applied strategically and carefully. The Lord allowed Moses to view the promised land without entering it (Num. 27:12–14; Deut. 34:1–8). Jehovah took special care to even bury Moses Himself in a place not known to anyone. God did not strip this faithful servant of his validity, not in any way. Despite a mistake, this dear man was treasured and honored. God, in His wisdom, instilled what modern society has named as succession planning. In agreement with His dear servant, Joshua was chosen before Moses's demise. The Lord had Moses significantly lay his hands on Joshua, imparting some of the honor that Moses possessed onto this young man, his successor (Num. 27:15–23; Deut. 34:9–12).

The saga of Moses reflects Jehovah's leadership in many forms. It shows a leader who foresees a subject's potential. This is often, way beyond what the person may see within themselves. Within this saga is the importance of communication. The "face-to-face" audiences of Moses and the Lord were valuable investments for desired yields and outcomes (Ex. 33:11–17). The Lord exemplifies a leader who has a formulated plan ahead of time, before His initial audience with the chosen vessel (person). Also seen is a leader who is willing to revise their plan when credible input is received from those involved. The Lord also shows leadership that does not just give a plan and then abandon the project. Rather than one that abandons, He travels through the project, not micromanaging but still on hand for consultation and approval when needed. This leadership promotes the serious importance of acknowledgment and reward.

Another subject that displays the leadership of Almighty God is the account of Gideon. The record of this mighty man opens with the overwhelming patience of the Supreme Being toward Gideon. Gideon is a representative of those who have been beaten down by life. In this state, they are reluctant to even think that things can change. They have low self-esteem and distrust. The perception that they own is that if anything can be done, surely they are not capable of having a part in it (Judg. 6:11–40). The angel of the Lord addressed Gideon as to what was in him and what he would be, not how Gideon saw himself (Judg.6:12). This vessel had his excuses flowing rather than accepting the assignment and challenge to be the deliverer. God's patience was tested when Gideon asked the angel for a sign and also twice with the fleece. A leader must be understanding and often meet people at the point where they are. The Lord also gave Gideon on-the-job training. This training would help him know how to read people, thus enabling him to assess those who would be faithful and diligent for the duration of the project. God's handling of this mighty man restored Gideon's faith in the Almighty God. The self-esteem of this man was greatly improved. A different view of life evolved from this experience. As with Moses, Jehovah reinforced to Gideon that He was with him. God renewed His servant's ability to trust by keeping His word and bringing His promises to fruition (Judg.7:1–25).

B. The Sovereign Leadership of God

The absolute, supreme leadership of God leaves no place for debate. Many decisions in life recorded in the biblical Scriptures show forth the unequivocal sovereignty of God. One of these examples that immediately comes to mind is the dilemma involving Esau and Jacob (Gen. 25:19, 28:9; Mal. 1:1–4; Rom. 9:9–21). So often, in one's human manner, it would seem entertaining to attempt to determine who righteously should be entitled to the birthright, but it cannot be truly determined. The events of Isaac's family and those surrounding his sons often seem to play out like a complex soap opera. All things considered, one has no other resolve but to acknowledge that all events were in the plan of God to bring forth His purpose and will. One truly would ask, Why cause Rebekah to strategically hear Isaac's request to Esau? Why did Isaac get tricked? Why cause Jacob to leave his home? Why is Esau in a disgruntled state? This guidance is the sovereign will of God. Such leading events were the patterned stones unfolding the plan of God.

As it has been established, a leader directs and guides one in the manner needed to accomplish the desired goal. However, the same approach to mannerism is not always feasible or a good fit for everyone across the board. Here the sovereignty of God comes into view with Moses and the circumcision of his son (Ex. 4:24–26). Even though God had spoken to Moses from the place of the burning bush (Ex. 3:1–14), there is no respect of persons. God seemingly would have killed him because of the covenant and circumcision (Gen. 17:9–14; Josh. 5:3–9). Therefore, Jehovah is the God of protocol and of covenant, no matter the individual, yet He is merciful.

Before leaving this area, it is fitting to speak of Jesus as the servant-leader—the One who initiates His relation with the disciples through being hospitable and inviting (Matt. 4:18–25; Jn. 1:39). He would be found to serve not only with food but also by washing feet (Jn. 13:1–17). This Master would travel to heal (Matt. 9:18–26). The Lord could comprehend the frustration of Zacchaeus and meet his needs (Lk. 19:1–10). He had compassion for the multitudes and taught and directed means to feed them spiritually and literally. The account of Lazarus shows perceptions of family, friendship, loss, and ministry (Jn. 11:1–46). As seen and recorded in the gospels, Jesus carefully and steadily prepared His disciples, the apostles, for the time after His ascension. He mindfully gave them their assignment, instructions, and the message that should be dispersed (Matt. 28:16–20; Lk. 24:36–53). Jesus prepared His followers to move in faith, believing the unbelievable. Steward and Mann have stated, "This can be difficult in the face of what appears to be certain failure or defeat. But to succeed in following the example of Christ, servant-leaders must be willing to look beyond his or her circumstances."[9]

C. Leadership of The New Testament Church

The leadership of the church in the New Testament rested mainly on the shoulders of the apostles. These leaders were born

---

[9]   David L. Steward, Brandon K. Mann, *Leadership by the Good Book* (New York: Faith Words/Hachette Book Group Inc., 2020), 214

from the apostles and disciples (others) that abode in the upper room. This upper-room occupancy occurred after the resurrection and ascension of Jesus Christ. On the day of Pentecost, these occupants were abiding in one accord. They all experienced being filled with the Holy Ghost and speaking in other tongues. Such expression was as the Spirit gave them utterance (Acts 2: 1–47). Although these occupants impacted the world, certain key apostles are looked upon as outstanding leaders. These key figures would emerge at the forefront of this movement, thought of as the "New Testament Church." The very significant apostles were namely Peter and Philip, who were in the upper room, and Paul, who joined afterward (Acts 8:4–8, 9:1–22, 17:1–30; Rom. 11:13). Peter is known mainly as the one who addressed the Jews and those in the Jerusalem area. Philip is noted as the one who witnessed in Judaea and Samaria, addressing the Samaritans. Lastly, Apostle Paul is the one who witnessed to the uttermost part of the earth, addressing the Gentiles and all those that would listen.

The leadership of Peter sprung forth on the day of Pentecost. He spoke out and delivered his first and very powerful sermon. The magnitude of what happened that day resulted in thousands of souls receiving the message of salvation. Such souls were added to the church on that day. The Lord caused the church to increase daily. Peter did not exemplify fear but boldness in defending the faith. He showed how he was in tune with the Holy Spirit. Being in tune with and obedient to God was evident in Peter's encounter with Cornelius (Acts 10:1–48).

Under the guidance of the Holy Spirit, Peter was strongly directed to understand that the gospel needed to be inclusive of all people. The thoughts and actions of this apostle needed to be and were revised to promote inclusion. However, Peter further along needed to be corrected again concerning this issue. He was rebuffed by Paul for leaning toward exclusion again rather than inclusion. This concerned the Jews and the Gentiles and the issue of circumcision (Gal. 2:11–20). Peter, in this instance, allowed external forces and behaviors to influence his actions and responses to those he would be ministering to. One's human nature can have great influence and weight on actions in and out of ministry, which would seem to be the lesson here in leadership. Peter can be viewed, for the most part, as being solid as a rock. He possessed tenacity and boldness, whether facing opposition or persecution (Matt. 16:18–19).

Philip, an apostle and one of the twelve disciples that walked with Jesus, did spread the gospel in Judaea and Samaria (Acts 8:5). He was the one who ministered to the Ethiopian eunuch (Acts 8:26–40). This same Philip was also the one who simply requested of Jesus, "Lord, shew us the Father, and it sufficeth us" (John 14:7–12). For this, Philip received Jesus's reprimand and admonishment. Philip, although not seemingly as prominent as Peter and Paul, was active serving in the ministry. It is believed he was one of the first deacons who served alongside Stephen (Acts 6:1–7). There are some who entertain the thought that it may have been another Philip as deacon though. Philip, noted as an evangelist, is also accounted for as hosting Paul's company at his home. This is recorded as happening during Paul's third missionary journey (Acts 21:8). This apostle, even though he is not as prominent as his comrades, is consistent in doing his part in fulfilling the assigned mission (Acts 1:8). Philip was a man of remarkable character. Tichy and Bennis note the importance of character, leaders, and judgment and say of character:

> It means having a moral compass that sets clear parameters for what one will, and will not do. Character is all about knowing right from wrong and having worked these issues out long before facing tough judgment calls. It is about knowing what your goals and standards are and sticking with them.[10]

In conjunction with Philip, the deacon Stephen must be spoken of as an example of the leadership of the growing foundational church. Stephen was chosen as one of the first deacons, the group of

---

[10] Noel M. Tichy and Warren G. Bennis, *Judgment: How Winning Leaders Make Great Calls* (New York: Penguin Group, 2007), 70

"seven men of honest report, full of the Holy Ghost and wisdom" (Acts 6:3–7). Stephen was a powerful representative of the gospel. Many miracles and wonders were performed by him. This deacon was the recipient of the third persecution of the church (Acts 6:8–15). His dialogue with certain members of the synagogue infuriated them. Stephen was brought before the council and addressed the unbelief of Israel. The result of this address was that Stephen became the first martyr of the early church. Stephen's fortitude and faith are an established icon of the church. His gentleness in facing death as he was stoned is a memorial (Acts 7:54–60).

Lastly, the other outstanding leader of the early church was Paul—this Paul, who was known as Saul prior to his conversion and his Damascus road experience (Acts 9:1–17, 13:9). Luke, the writer of Acts, was careful to note that Saul, prior to his conversion, was in the company of Stephen's persecutors. Also, this leader was present at the stoning and death of Stephen. Saul was an aggressive and ardent persecutor of the early church (Acts 8:1–3). The conversion of this apostle, known as Saul and Paul (Acts 13:9), is a major point in the history of the early church. Significantly, Paul's conversion caused him to become a crusader for the gospel. He did this with the same or more intense fervor than he had when he persecuted the church. Paul had a personal and direct encounter with the Lord on the road to Damascus.

Paul was Christ's witness who could not be stopped or subdued. He fulfilled the assignment to the uttermost part of the earth (Acts 1:8). He was not confined to Jerusalem but launched his missionary journeys often from Antioch. As a result of his evangelism and pastoring, many churches were established. Churches established in Rome, Corinth, Galatia, Ephesus, Philippi, Colosse, and Thessalonica received from him as he was guided by the Lord. Some received commendation, while others received correction. He nurtured and admonished the flock of Christ through his visitations and also by means of his many letters, known as epistles. Paul evidenced that communication is a key part of all that one does and attempts to do (1 Cor. 16:1–24; Eph. 6:21–24; Col. 4:7–18). Whether by action, script, vocally, or modern-day technology, this factor helps everyone to be involved and hopefully get on board with the goal desired.

Paul nurtured and poured into Timothy much. He took him as a spiritual son (1 Tim. 1:1–2). With Timothy, he desired to have him fully prepared for ministry, pastoring, and life. This preparation occurred not only at the time of Paul's presence and life, but more so after he would no longer be around or alive. His letters to Timothy in First and Second Timothy give guidance, blueprints for behavior, clear instructions, and also encouragement. He takes diligent effort to stir this young man who would succeed him. He admonishes him also to not be hampered by his youth but rather to be an example of the believers (1 Tim. 4:12). This apostle reminded Timothy of his heritage. Paul admonished him to endure and to be mindful of what he had learned. He reiterated the need to study, teach, and cherish the holy scriptures (1 Tim. 4:10–16; 2 Tim. 2:15–19, 3:14–17). As a good leader, Paul reinforced to Timothy to be consistent (2 Tim. 4:1–5). Thus, in this current time, such an example is pristine to follow.

D. Leadership of the Seven Churches of Revelation

As the Apostle John was commanded to write down the vision seen (Rev. 1:19–20), there would be messages within this vision. The messages from the glorified risen Lord Jesus Christ were to the angels of the seven churches. The seven stars were symbolic of these angels, who were regarded as the pastors of the noted churches. Each church had characteristics unique to itself. The churches noted were: Ephesus, Smyrna, Pergamos, Thyatira, Sardis, Philadelphia, and Laodicea. Basically, the messages received were, for the most part, either that of commendation or condemnation. Those of condemnation served as warnings to the specific pastors so that they might correct their errors. Commendation would be more so believed to serve as reinforced support and encouragement of favored behaviors and results.

To the pastor of the church of Ephesus, a message of condemnation was addressed. This church was written as having left its first love. Subsequently, the label given here was that of a backslidden church. The suggested action is to return to its first love and do its first works again (Rev. 2:1–7). There is acknowledgment of the good work done. The hatred of those professing falsely, that are liars. This is deemed commendable, along with hatred of the deeds of the Nicolaitans. Such deeds were of loose morals, idol involvement, and the like. The pastor-leader here is implored to repent, do first works over again, get back to the beginning, and get the passion for the Lord back in his life. Thus, in all likelihood, the congregation would follow. The reward will be to partake of the tree of life, which is in the midst of the paradise that belongs to God.

The pastor of Smyrna receives no complaints or condemnation. On the other hand, this leader is the recipient of commendations. Christ, the first and the last, is pleased with their unfailing faithfulness in the midst of tribulation, poverty, and persecution (Rev. 2:8–11). This church has been branded as a suffering church. The example is set here to be faithful in the midst of any storm or circumstance. If one steps back from Smyrna, there is still the example and reference that are to be seen in the man, Job (The Book of Job). In leadership, ministry, business, scholastics, at home, and friends, one is encouraged and strongly urged to be faithful: faithful to one's faith in God Almighty; faithful to the values, principles, and morals that are held so dear; faithful to the task that one has signed on to do and see through to the end, and that with excellence; and faithful to one's brethren, fellow coworkers, family, neighbors, and friends. There is a reward in store. For the church of Smyrna, it is the crown of life, also known as the martyr's crown. For one's purpose, it is to be the reflection of the divine in the home, the workplace, and as well as in the sanctuary. Concerning suffering, T. D. Jakes takes space to express:

> When we suffer, we seek answers. Perhaps it's the desire to regain some semblance of control over circumstances that remind us of our utter powerlessness in certain realities. Or maybe it's just our human longing to believe that everything happens for a reason, that all the details of our lives should fit together like puzzle pieces

revealing significance beyond anything we can see from our surface perspective.

For those of us who trust in the goodness and sovereignty of God, this compelling need to understand why certain events occur is no less stringent. "And we know that in all things God works for the good..." (Rom. 8:28). Even as we cling to the promises of divine truth, we scrutinize our natural world for answers that can only have supernatural solutions. Somehow we inherently believe that if we can understand the motivation and contextualization of our crisis, then we can contain it, reduce it, eliminate it.[11]

The leadership of the church of Pergamos was addressed with commendation as well as condemnation (Rev. 2:12–17). This church had been categorized as a licentious church. Although it was good in holding fast to the name of Christ and not denying the faith, there were yet some unfavorable issues. The issues presented themselves as compromise. Coinciding with their holding fast and the faith, they permitted the allowance of the doctrines of Balaam and the Nicolaitans. These compromising doctrines gave credence to compromised morality and encouraged adultery and fornication. In addition, with such compromise, the gateway to eating food sacrificed to idols and erroneous teachings was launched. The angel of this church was warned to repent or bear the consequences. One is admonished to be vigilant, personally and in organizations, in order to assess and be aware of compromise that contaminates. It is wise to review one's foundational principles. After review, take time to measure where one stands or lines up and correct as needed. Know the portrayal that is being presented and whether it is true to form. Conflicting values do not tend to provide a healthy existence (Jam. 3:11–18).

---

[11] T. D. Jakes, *Crushing* (New York: Faith Words/Hachette Book Group Inc., 2019), 57

Thyatira's angel received commendation from the Lord for their patience, love, service, faith, and works. However, the message of condemnation was due to their being tainted by allowing the contrariness of Jezebel and her teaching (Rev. 2:18–29). Also, the committing of fornication and eating that which was sacrificed to idols were noted against this church. As with Pergamos, the wrong compromise is not good. The pastor here was warned to repent. If repentance was heeded, the specific promise to be received was in place. In the message of Thyatira, it is noted that everyone will receive according to their works (Rev. 2:23). Therefore, one should strive to do justly, be honest, and be diligent in whatever is done, giving forth one's best ability (Eph. 6:5–8; Col. 3:22–25).

The angel of the church in Sardis was informed that God considered this church dead (Rev. 3:1–6). There is no commendation given; however, there is notation that some exist that have not defiled their garments (Rev. 3:4). Sardis has received warnings and promises. It is possible for one to think they are alive and doing well when, in reality, they're dead, dying, and just haven't laid down yet. A spiritually dead leader may have one operating with a form of godliness without the power thereof (2 Tim. 3:5). When one feels that they can do all for themselves, they are prone to trust in possessions and their own strength, and God is out of the picture or mix. There is no viable relationship with God. In one's personal life, business, or organization, this type of state may be evidenced by a lack of love or care for others. Also, the leader may be spiritually asleep or in business, being unengaged commercially. Prayer may be lacking, along with compliance with the word of God. The person, while functioning in the land of the living, has the opportunity or chance to reverse this state. The leader here must see this and acknowledge the truth of the matter. Then thereafter, strategize and apply the corrective action. It starts with a majority of one.

To the angel/pastor of the church in Philadelphia, the message comes with commendation. The Lord knows the work of these (Rev. 3:7–13). The acknowledgment is that they have a little strength with which they have kept Christ's word and not denied His name. This church is actively in revival. Philadelphia is encouraged to hold fast so that no one takes their crown (Rev. 3:11). Their promise is given if they overcome. This seems to be exemplary of an organization or person that has things going well with the right focus and relationship. Nevertheless, with everything proceeding well, it is good to be grateful and continue to move forward watchfully, not in fear. Continuing to keep one's focus on the right goals and relationships so as not to lose out in the end (Isa. 26:3).

The message to Laodicea is the seventh and last to the churches. Laodicea was declared to have a lukewarm status, neither hot nor cold. Such is indicative of one who feels self-sufficient, has increased wealth and goods, and is in need of nothing. However, God perceives this one as wretched, miserable, poor, blind, and naked (Rev. 3:14–19). The message implies that this church is still loved. The Lord affirms that those whom He loves are rebuked, chastened, and given the chance to repent. The warning comes in the hope of deferring and preventing judgment. The promise stands for those who will hear and apply revision. Hence, this will be a mending of their ways (Rev. 3:20–22). In business, organization, or life, an evidenced positive change in productivity is likely to ensue.

CHAPTER 5

Modern-Day Leadership

A. In the Secular Sector

Modern-day leadership, in some ways, may draw from the framework of yesteryear. However, major enhancements and technology have added much more. The focus seems to stay the same. Most are concerned with wealth and health. Since the COVID-19 pandemic, the overall population has been traumatized and is in a state of recovery. Death has been experienced in great quantity worldwide in such a short span of time. Leadership has had to redefine itself somewhat. The shift and redesign have had to find ways to factor in urgent cares of life. Many struggled with attacks on their health, both physical and mental. These struggles thrust many into unfamiliar territory. Major chunks of society had to deal with loss of income and, for some, loss of home and shelter. A major concern had to do with forms of isolation and the effects thereof. Major goals emerging from this new way of life were the creation of means for communication, livelihood, food, and daily care.

Leadership instituted daily briefing sessions, communicating the rapidly changing results of the pandemic. The results of viral activity and severity were and are communicated, as are the responses of the government, medical staff and facilities, and community. Plans were sketched out to reach out to those who could not help themselves. Checking in on the elderly and door-to-door food provisions were offered at crucial intervals. Although some businesses failed, others restructured themselves and survived. Because of restrictions on consumer activity, some enterprises literally had no recourse but to close. Management-leadership in some enterprises chose to shift their resources to others, combine, and collaborate to stay viable. Companies that could choose and institute means by which their employees were able to work remotely did so, and this action supported two major efforts. The effort of keeping known staff employed was one. The other effort was continuity of customer and client services, which helped individually, community-wise, and corporately.

Another phase of modern leadership operates in the scholastic realm. In this post-pandemic time, many changes have launched. Mandates were given, communicated, and enforced that totally prevented in-person contact for a long interval. Long-established routines were drastically interrupted. Educators, administrators, funders, parents and family, health officials, and technicians all had to bring their skills together. This collaboration helped to continue the education efforts and keep students connected and engaged. Relevancy for all ages and subjects had to be applied to these efforts. The accomplishment of the goals desired was measured through observation, evaluation, and feedback. The leadership in these areas revised the different products as needed. Revision adjustments were and still are applied as societal changes happen. Rutland says, "In the systems-analysis phase of a turnaround, look for what you *do* have. Anyone can see the challenges. A visionary leader must see the opportunities and creative ways to leverage resources."[12]

Leaders, for the sake of making things truly work, must take the responsibility to accept the different ideas that may come their way. Upon seeking continued improved productivity, the avenue for new and different approaches must be open and available to receive input. Positive leadership welcomes input and creativity from all parties and players. On the subject of change, Norton expresses, "*Creativity* has to do with the proposal, development, and implementation of new

---

[12] Mark Rutland, *ReLaunch* (Colorado Springs: David C. Cook, 2013), 77

and better solutions while productivity is the efficient application of current solutions…the capacity to exercise a relatively high degree of imagination, ingenuity, and creativity…is widely, not narrowly, distributed in the population."[13]

B. In the Family

The modern family structure has varied and diverted somewhat from the traditional model. Leadership of the family unit in some cases and families has shifted. Such a shift has been influenced by the media and society. Single-parent homes have shaken the framework of parenting. At times, because of obligations of employment, church, and community, decisions for the family are determined with weighty input from children and parents. Prior to this shift, traditional decisions were made by the father figure solely or with input from the mother, if at all. Today's society seems to strongly advocate and encourage input from the children of the family for life decisions. Despite this modern mode of behavior, there are some families that have chosen to hold fast to traditional teachings, customs, and ceremonies.

Many Jewish families seem to be ardent about consistently carrying on the traditions and rituals of their fathers and forefathers. The importance and value of legacy in some other cultures are not always evident. Those that have glimpsed at the value thereof have turned to the ancestry search engines to get them help. With the ancestry finds, some have reached out to distant relatives. Here they have traced family trees in the hope of some guidance, foundation, and stability. Modern families at times seem to be functioning with wavering leadership, which may be assessed as a form of dysfunction. Absent parents, because of imprisonment or voluntary abandonment, leave the guidance to an older sibling, an alternate relative, or the social system.

---

[13] M. Scott Norton, *Dealing with Change* (Lanham: Rowman & Littlefield, 2018), 109

Yet there are still some today who have chosen to live life according to biblical teachings and principles, for the most part. One can possibly recall certain standards held within their immediate home. Whether or not such standards were upheld in other relatives' homes did not matter as far as one was concerned. These standards were a code of ethics to be held to and practiced wheresoever one might be. What comes to mind in this area are the directives given to the children of Israel (Deut. 6:4–7). Just this short snippet from the full passage gives a standard for living, leadership, and legacy. By loving God, one thus has a benchmark that rises up within one's character. Through consistently teaching specific values to one's children, they become a way of life in most instances. There are writings that echo clearly, "Children learn what they live."

Many scenarios come to mind when thinking of the influence of leadership in one's family. A biblical account that may seem random is the exact action that Isaac took with Rebekah in Gerar (Gen. 26:1–11). This did seem to mirror Abraham's actions with Sarah in the same Gerar and concerning Abimelech (Gen. 20: 1–18). Both patriarchs reverted to claiming that "his wife was his sister." It is interesting to note that Isaac was not even born when Abraham had such an encounter. There is no specific account to imply that he was schooled to react as thus. Yet one must ponder whether or not such an inclination was in the genes, nurtured in the environment of development, or possibly both. Somewhere along his life's road, Isaac was guided. Truly, his guidance can be attributed not only to his biological father but even more so to his heavenly Father.

A reflection in this same area of thought concerning the family is the collection of informal, casual, meaningful proverbs shared by parents throughout one's lifetime. In the home and with others, one may observe parental generosity, kindness, and patience. A patriarchal proverb at times given was that, in ministry especially, one must be willing to "spend and be spent." The interpretation here seems to be convoluted between God's call and self-sacrifice. Either one of these consciously requires something from an individual, and above all, their willingness to give of themselves. The generosity here would seem to reflect that of scriptural guidance (Deut. 15:10; Matt. 5:42–48; Lk. 6:30–36).

It's amazing how a parent can take a simple activity in daily living and make it a lesson for life. One recalls an ordinary drive with one's father and the instructions given as guidance for driving and for life. At this time, one's father casually shared, yet with a stern sense, that one is responsible for always having their vehicle under control. This seemed to even imply that of one's vessel also. The understanding here would strongly imply that regardless of what is happening around one, one should not have their responsibilities contribute to the confusion or chaos (Prov. 16:32; Eph. 6:1–4, 6–7; Phil. 2:12; 2 Thess. 3:11–15).

Thoughts of family leadership surely would seem to include a daily Bible study, a scripture verse, or a selection from the book of Proverbs. An imbedded desire nurtured here would be to strive to be wise (Prov. 18:1–4, 12–16, 21, 24). A mother here would take the opportunity at one time to ask her child, "Do you have any initiative?" This can prompt one to begin a journey of thinking "out of the box" and searching for ways to make whatever it is better (Col. 3:14–17). Such thoughts would be enhanced by a dear uncle's mantra of "Good, better, best; Never let it rest; Till your good gets better; And your better is best!" These words would prove to be a pattern to live by, yielding excellent results (Prov. 18:16). Excellent results are not only what such pearls of wisdom generate. These pearls also fuel a passion that promotes and propels one's work ethics not only to men but even more so to God (Ps. 19:9–11, 37:3–5; Prov. 3:1–10, 9:9–11, 16:3, 9, 22:6; Col. 3:17, 23–24).

In the light of such reflections, one recalls a mother as a woman of faith. In my recollection, there is an account of a young woman in the era when being married by a certain age or stage in life was paramount; she had no prospects in view, not one in sight. Distressed and distraught, coupled with parental innuendoes and pressure, she put her plight and request before the Lord. With what she believed was her answer and no physical prospect in view, she proceeded to plan her wedding. What comes to mind here is Abraham and Jehovah-Jireh, "God will provide" (Gen. 22:7–14). Truly, God did provide her mate, a pristine candidate, in perfect timing. They were noted for actively living out their marital vows with joy and happiness. This spanned a length of time reaching over fifty-five and a half years, literally until death us do part. Interestingly enough, their lives together mirrored, or rather echoed, the well-rehearsed scripture in the biblical book of Ruth. The verse that says, "Intreat me not to leave thee, or to return from following after thee: for whither thou goest, I will go; and where thou lodgest, I will lodge: thy people shall be my people, and thy God my God: Where thou diest, will I die, and there will I be buried: the LORD do so to me, and more also, if ought but death part thee and me" (Ruth 1:16–17).

This couple set and lived an example for their children as well as others. Here, the witness of two becoming one was evident in one's daily life (Gen. 2:24; Mk. 10:6–9). These two faced many joys, challenges, and rewards together. At one point in their lives, when they concluded that they needed someplace better to raise their family, they chose to step out in faith again. According to the account, they did not selfishly venture out by themselves. They, however, encouraged another couple that was having the same experience to take a leap and go forward. With less than what would be the cost of a fast-food meal in this day and time, each couple put a binder of five dollars on their individual prospected house to be their home. These houses were then being built in a new development.

Different circumstances in people's lives produce different outcomes, some reaching in totally opposite directions. However, for the couple originally venturing forth on such a leap of faith, that minimal investment has multiplied multiple times with God's blessings upon it. The scripture that comes to mind is that of faithfulness, whether it is little or when it is not even yours (Luke 16: 10–12). Also, what can be noted here is a message from Proverbs, that of a man leaving an inheritance for his family (Psa. 112:1–9, 128:1–6; Prov. 10:22, 13:22). It would be right to note that one's parents believed and practiced the "law" of giving tithes and offerings freely to the Lord. This seemed to be a foundational statute without wavering. A practice and custom that they taught their children by their living. They openly admonished not only their children and grandchildren on the blessings of tithing and giving but others all around them in their life's circle (Lev. 27:30–33; 1 Chron. 16:25–29; Psa. 96:5–8; Prov. 3:1–10; Hag. 1:5–13; Mal. 3:8–12; Lk. 6:38; 2 Cor. 9:6–11). Faith and these actions do partner with the writings of Steve Gladen as he expressed, "more about faith in following the leading of the Holy Spirit than the careful and strategic planning of a single man…This bold faith is foundational…to all we do. If we believe God is leading, the dream is never too big—never impossible."[14]

In one's home, lying and stealing were not condoned. A gracious mother would instruct, "If you'll lie, you'll steal. If you'll steal, you'll commit murder." No one in their right mind wants to go down such a slippery slope. The best thing to gather from here would be not to practice lying, case and point (Psa. 120:2). Truth spoken in season and out of season was the preferential protocol (Jn. 8:32; Phil. 4:8–9). The thought of stealing just did not seem to be an issue. General behavior was to have bedroom doors unlocked and open. The home did not operate with cloak and dagger, locking doors, hiding and securing pocketbooks, handbags, piggy banks, wallets, etc. There seems to be no need for that. Monies could be placed out on the table or in the open within the home and remain fully accountable. However, in some other venues, homes, and around some other people, this was not the norm (1 Tim. 6:10–12). A wise woman would train her children and grandchildren to be around money and know how to be trusted. They would be fully aware where money bags were and, at times, sent to get them without a twinge (Eph. 6:1–7).

As one pauses at this juncture to reflect on what defines family at times, family can be considered a group of people united by some common element such as association, affiliation, or even affliction. Thus, thinking in this realm, one considered the family, leadership, and executive-type decisions surrounding the account of the four lepers (2 Kgs. 7:3–20). Sometimes in life, desperate times call for desperate measures. In the lives of this "leprous family" of four men, several components of leadership exemplified themselves. Some of

---

[14] Steve Gladen, *Small Groups with Purpose* (Grand Rapids: Baker Books, 2011), 25

the components observed were assessment, unification, the design of a plan, and execution thereof. In addition to these components, love as charity and community concern, along with communication, are all well seen. The lepers assessed that they literally had nothing to lose if they stayed at their present place. The projected evaluation was that their end would be inevitable. Thus, weighing the law of averages, the decision to be proactive and get up and move went into effect. Their movement appeared to be divinely orchestrated and favored by God. Even though their decision's outcome proved favorable, they chose not to hoard for themselves only but rather to have compassion (Matt. 22:37–39) and share. As a result, the members of this family were instrumental in relieving suffering and bringing deliverance. Their actions helped not only in their dire situation but also in the deliverance of so many others.

Dwelling in this segment, one remembers the leadership guidance given by the patriarch. This guidance did not always come in the form of rules, but often in what could be considered idioms of wisdom. From these idioms, one was encouraged to glean understanding, use application, and watch, thereby observing the effect. Along with this, one might possibly refer to a current account, happening, observation, or biblical account and reference. An idiom such as "The eye of the master fattens the beast" would more so have the meaning that one needs to be actively present in operations. Not present to micromanage but more so to show interest and, when appropriate, be a part of the team. This tends to breed accountability, commitment, and excellence in the execution of tasks. In modern-day worksites, this might be comparable to the executive doing occasional visits to the loading docks, factory floors, etc. This also needs to be coupled with getting to know one's employees, workers, staff, etc. with a sincere interest in one's people. One should have relatively good knowledge and understanding of what's going on in the overall operations, large or small, and those involved. This can be applied to the home as well as the corporate scene and even the church.

As one continues to write and read in this portion of leadership, one becomes more and more aware of the magnitude of the effect that one's father and his words have on one's life. One must believe that such a combination was enhanced by the infusion of a mother's words echoing, "So teach us to number our days, that we may apply our hearts unto wisdom" (Psa. 90:12). What this might encourage is that if one is not on a wisdom journey already, then one's journey needs to start today and go forward. Also, in one's family, the importance of communion was set forth. Not meaning communion as the holy sacrament but more so that of fellowship found at the dining table. Think here of Christ with His disciples and again with Zacchaeus (Matt. 9:10–13; Lk. 19:1–10; Jn. 21:9–17). Eating meals together fosters a time to share. This sharing can be literal, as sharing food for variety, or for concern in that everyone gets their needed portion. Here one might lightly think on the account of the loaves and the fishes (Matt. 14:17–21, 15:32–38; Mk. 6:37–44, 8:1–9; Lk. 9:10–17; Jn. 6:1–13).

The account of the children of Israel and their daily portion of manna in the wilderness is also thought of as the reassuring consistent provision of one's parent-leader (Ex. 16; Deut. 8:3). Sharing here can also be inclusive of a recap of the events of the day and offer a time of release, commendation, and, if necessary, gentle correction. This sharing time is also a monumental opportunity for teaching and applying table manners and dining protocol. One may not realize the tremendous value of this practice until one visits a home where it is nonexistent. It seems almost devastating to observe a family where each member randomly comes, gets, or grabs the food prepared and goes to their individual rooms or television. No connection, communion, or cohesiveness was seen here. Sadly, that appeared to be just how such a family lived their lives.

True leadership in a family provides foundational pillars that aid its members throughout life's journey. Good leadership most often tends to be proactive rather than reactive. This approach was very often what one's parents believed was the best action concerning most matters. Proactivity could be applied to issues of behavior, like a small leak somewhere or a leaky faucet, a crack in the ceiling, educational preparation, a tear in a garment, an occasional malfunctioning vehicle, etc. The proverbial statements offered in some of these instances might vary from "A stitch in time saves nine" or "An ounce of prevention is worth a pound of cure" to "Let's nip this in the bud." Whatever the situation, these statements meant that something definitely needed to be addressed.

In some cases, it may have meant that what was being produced was not good and would not be tolerated. Therefore, let us get it corrected now so that future production will yield a desirable outcome. If, perchance, the situation involved a behavioral issue, it then might have further accompaniment. The accompaniment chosen was very possibly found in the Proverbs of the Bible. Delightful verses such as, "He that spareth his rod hateth his son: but he that loveth him chasteneth him betimes" (Prov. 13:24); "Train up a child in the way he should go: and when he is old, he will not depart from it" (Prov. 22:6); or "Foolishness is bound in the heart of a child; but the rod of correction shall drive it far from him" (Prov. 22:15), may have been the accompaniment given with love. In thinking of love, one should embrace Proverbs 3 and some of its specific verses (Prov. 3:1–14). To be clear, there was not any abuse but rather constructive explanatory discipline that yielded children and grandchildren of favorable promise.

There are times in life and in leadership when things just don't seem to go right. More accurately stated, "as one would think they should go." One might think that "the verdict" isn't fair or right. This might be seen in a squabble amongst siblings, in external relationships, or maybe in a transaction. At such times, when needful and fitting, a wise, peaceful, man of integrity patriarch would give words that truly were deep and carried consolation coupled with promise. Some words uttered were "Suffer it to be so now." These words seem to be applicable to many circumstances in life. The application of this statement seemed so relevant when one was frustrated and stressed. Especially in times of stress when someone seemed to have gotten the upper hand unlawfully, these words proved helpful. Such words helped to breed forgiveness within one for the perpetrator. On the other hand, these same words, "Suffer it to be so," were soothing to the individual who just could not do any better with the immediate resources that they had at the time.

A father's gently kind words would consent to the understanding that one is dealing with poor, underprivileged sources and/or materials, but be patient. The thought that one cannot do any better with what one has to work with, but when the circumstances change for the better, and they will, we all know that one will do better and improve. Thus, one develops patience and tolerance through the application of thoughtful understanding (Psa. 37:1–9; Rom. 12:9–21; Eph. 4:1–3; Phil. 4:5–7; Jas. 1:3–5). One realizes over and over again that quite a bit of their familial guidance was philosophical. To "Suffer it to be so now," the words "The mills of God grind slowly, but exceedingly fine" were sometimes added. "The mills…" would seem to be a variation of the philosophical and poetic words of Sextus Empiricus, Sun Tzu, and Henry Wadsworth. These words would truly implicate that judgment and justice will eventually come forth.

In reflection or retrospection, one might truly believe that, unconsciously, these philosophical words influenced one's behavior and outcome in their adult workplace. Even though it may seem hard sometimes, be not weary in well-doing (Gal. 6:9). One experienced the repercussions of a jealous coworker who incited opposition in the workplace. This insurrection resulted in a supervisory ruling that had to be given, though unwillingly because of restraints. Consistently doing what one knows is right, no matter the present outcome, prevails (Col. 3:22–24). The opposing individual was later found in varied compromising situations on their own account. Such occurrences resulted in the supervisor's adamant reversal of the ruling. In circumstances like these, when others have sided with the opposition, one may think of Julius Caesar's "et tu, Brute." However, it becomes even more necessary to apply the Joseph-type aspect of forgiveness (Gen. 42–45).

As one can see, the words and presence of a father have a long-reaching effect. However, the leadership input of a father may come through the genes, through reflections and stories about the parent, and even in the lifetime that houses the father's absence. Many have witnessed the immense leadership skills of Barack Obama. Yet, from his memoirs and written accounts, his father appeared not to be physically present in his life most of the time. Nevertheless, it would seem that his father's values, tenacity, confidence, hope, and fortitude to navigate change for the betterment of people impacted him greatly. Barack noted, "At the time of his death, my father remained a myth to me, both more and less than a man."[15] One might assess that this example of leadership and the familial impact, although somewhat "unorthodox," still yielded a most favorable outcome.

In a comparative look, Randy Brown seems to advocate that a father's presence is paramount. He states:

> I truly believe there are blessings designated for a father to impart to his children. These are blessings a father can release from his spirit, from his overseer/headship position (if you would like to call it that), into the lives of his children to be able to send them into realms of success and prosperity, blessings, guidance, and breakthroughs. In order for his children's lives to be orchestrated so that positive change can take place, I believe the father must be involved in their lives… Fathers need to be vocal…The influence and the importance of the position of that father are very necessary to the operation…He wants that child to hit the mark, not just once in their life but many times.[16]

One would believe that to have such a definitive shaping of a child's life, a father would need to have a hands-on approach and be actively present. Not only in current times is this true, but on a biblical and spiritual platform, this is also proven. In the case of Abraham, Jehovah God, the ultimate Father, instructed Abraham to move away from his kindred and the house of Terah, his biological father (Gen. 12:1), thereby breaking the influence of Terah, an idol

---

[15] Barack Obama, *Dreams from My Father* (New York: Crown Publishers of Random House Inc., 2004), 5

[16] Randy Brown, *Blessings of a Father* (Lake Mary: Creation House, A Strang Company, 2006), 1, 24, and 38

worshipper, and the grips of idolatry. Abraham, likewise, influenced Isaac as they went to worship (Gen. 22). He further had a hands-on role, even in his old age, in the process of choosing the right wife for his son, Isaac (Gen. 24). The Apostle Paul throughout the Pauline Epistles displays the needful presence of a spiritual father. His relationship with Timothy, his spiritual son, is exemplary (1 Tim. 1:1–2). From the importance of the laying on of hands to his deeply rooted lineage in the faith, Paul made Timothy mindful of the greatness invested in him (2 Tim. 1:1–7). The apostle took effort to etch out every possible directive that his son would need to manage and fulfill his assignment as a young pastor. More so, not just to fulfill his assignment but to execute it with excellence (1 Tim. 4:11–16).

Continuing to think on the aspect of leadership in the family, the thought of guidance in timing comes about. The timing lessons learned can be applied to daily, personal, and even business life. In trying to acquire a certain station in life, human nature at times seeks to manipulate the process, causing disastrous effects. Other timing reflects one thrust into or seeking circumstances prematurely beyond their ability to handle such and doing this without divine guidance. What comes to mind here is a fatherly phrase that states, "If Greedy waits, hot will cool." Someone might pause and ponder what that phrase is all about, its true meaning, and the meaning behind it. Figuratively, one could possibly envision a somewhat cartoonish characterization of an anxious figure, too eager to partake of a meal item that is presently absolutely too hot to touch or consume. The likely outcomes of this scenario all seem undesirable. This hot item, too hot to handle, may drop and be damaged or even totally wasted and destroyed. If at all consumed, it may burn or hurt rather than be savored and enjoyed.

So what does this have to do with life? The answer to such a question is "The Ps," patience and preparation. Anxiously, life sometimes seems to be moving too slowly for the accomplishment of set or desired goals. On the other hand, one wants the vision or prophecy to happen now, not comprehending the whole "picture" or mechanism involved. Many noted biblical and experienced accounts support these truths. In the account of Abraham and Sarah concerning the prophecy of the son of promise (Gen. chapts. 15–18, 21), Abraham and Sarah attempted to manipulate the birth of the promised son. They interfered with what God had planned. Nevertheless, the Lord's plan prevailed. Their perception of when things should happen and their attempts to make them happen all caused regret and some problems. Problems that had to be addressed concerning Hagar and Ishmael.

The lesson of Greedy, patience, and preparation are seen in the account of the prodigal son (Lk. 15:11–32). The younger son (the prodigal) asks his father for his inheritance prematurely, and it is granted. This would be considered the "I want it now, and I don't want to wait" syndrome. In retrospect, this son had neither the wisdom, experience, nor maturity to handle what he was given at this stage of his life. The results, at first glance, appear disastrous. Nevertheless, the illustration of this parable reflects a father's overwhelming love and forgiveness. The assessment indicates the likelihood of poor outcomes when one is not sufficiently prepared to handle what they have. Fitting words from James, a servant of God (Jas. 1:1), seem appropriate to interject here. James says, "But let patience have her perfect work, that ye may be perfect and entire, wanting nothing. If any of you lack wisdom, let him ask of God, that giveth to all men liberally, and upbraideth not; and it shall be given him" (Jas. 1: 4–5). In a family, it is hoped that even when one messes up in life, whether at school, in careers, in relationships, etc., one can still come back home. Come back home and be received with open arms and love.

Greedy's lesson has so much to give in the way of guidance. One thinks of Peter, the disciple. He in himself thought that he could handle anything, any opposition, and not deny Christ, but he had never gone that way before, in terms of interrogation and the impending crucifixion (Matt. 26:33–35, 69–75; Mk. 14:29–31, 66–72; Lk. 22:31–34, 54–62; Jn. 13:36–38; 18:25–27). A parent as well as a leader tends to know their child's or the individual's frame, capabilities, true faults, shortcomings, and potential (Jn. 16:12–13). Likewise, Christ, having such closeness with Simon Peter, knew his weaknesses but also his future stamina and formidability. Peter, the work in progress, would shine forth after the crucifixion, resurrection, and upper room experience (Matt. 28:16–20; Lk. 24:1–12, 36–45, 49–53; Acts 1:3–9, 2:1–21).

Sometimes in a family and in parental-child relationships, it is not always what is said but more often what is not said in some instances. When children reach a certain level of adulthood, there comes the decision of living space. Some abruptly leave home without guidance or parental blessing, showing a lack of respect and honor (Ex. 20:12; Deut. 5:16; Matt. 15:4; Eph. 6:2). Some parents roughly aggravate their offspring, literally forcing them out of the familial domain as though they are not wanted (Eph. 6:4). This tends to breed long-lasting strained relationships that sometimes never heal. One experienced a unique outcome in this situation. After checking out an available prospect with seemingly good amenities, one shared and consulted with parents about the possibilities. There were no harsh demands, disapproval, or conditions offered by parents. They listened with slight smiles and an occasional chuckle, and then declared this would be great. Really great, because they expressed that they would have someplace to go with amenities and intended to utilize them. Besides that, they figured to be there when one came home from work, keeping a protective, watchful eye on their child while respecting the offspring's adulthood. Well, since respect and honor were mutual and well-established, it just didn't seem to have geography as the only added benefit. The best conclusion, which proved well, was to remain in the familial domain and wisely channel resources there while enjoying being surrounded by love.

Patience and preparation were lessons learned shortly after one acquired their driver's license in their early years. Fatherly input strongly suggested that one should first get their experience as a new driver on a used, a.k.a. pre-owned, vehicle rather than a new one. This was not just talk but shown interest and presence in shopping, choosing, and driving the right vehicle. Such input by the patriarch proved wise and beneficial. These actions fortify the relationships among family members and build a child's trust in their parents' wisdom, no matter how young or old they may be.

The presence of parents not only taught values but also the input of grandparents very much so too. Comically, going out with dear grandparents was somewhat of a military review indirectly, especially in the company of their friends. Here, one would be mindful to practice well-learned manners, politeness, respectful protocol, kindness, helpfulness, and being attentive to one's elders. These have proven to be lifelong cherished instructions. From these dear elders, one has also learned kindness, generosity, and initiative. Often, incorporated into grandparents' visitations and interactions were joyful laughter and family comedy. These tend to be the building blocks of a healthy adult life and are so valuable. Dr. Frank Thomas, in collaboration with T. D. Jakes has scrolled, "If we inherit, imitate, and mimic Grandma, we do not necessarily need a recipe, because we have her presence, example, demonstration, and conversation ever before us."[17]

C. In the Government/Judicial Sector

The leadership in government in this day and time seems guided by the personal agendas of the politicians. These agendas appear to be in the forefront of any docket rather than the needs of the people. In these pandemic times, however, mandates were aggressively put forth and enforced for the overall preservation of the general population. The government, during such crucial times, did step up and create measures to address health, economic, and survival needs. These measures visibly revealed that they provided ease and desired positive effects to respond to needs. Leadership in this sector seems to have a constant quarrel with the political parties involved. Often, the political players are in ongoing opposition. This opposition sometimes appears to be over issues that do not even make valid sense.

Moreover, as one may observe the logistics of today's democratic government, it would be interesting to note the leadership of government in biblical times and beyond. In narrowing this note with the

---

[17] T. D. Jakes with Dr. Frank Thomas, *Don't Drop the Mic* (New York: Faith Words Hachette Book Group, 2021), 337

hope of being concise, one may look at the branches of government with concentration mainly on one. The branches of government are known as judicial, legislative, and executive. For the purpose of notation, the concern here will be with the judicial sector of such an entity. When thinking about judicial, the components of judgment, judge, and justice are involved. In the Old Testament of the Bible, God is seen as the ultimate judge, especially concerning the children of Israel. The handbook for justice was etched in the biblical book of Leviticus.

God's messenger, as noted in Leviticus, is Moses, to whom He speaks from the tabernacle of the congregation (Lev. 1:1). Contrary to the judicial system of today, where the courts base their decisions on cases tried and ruled on, God's judgment is infinite. Divine warnings and judgments usually came by way of God's prophets (Num. 12:1–15; 2 Sam. 12:1–25). After Moses and Joshua, God allowed a series of judges to serve as leaders for the children of Israel (Judg. 1:1, 3:9; 1 Sam. 7:15, 8:1–6). The divine, theocratic leadership of Israel was snubbed by the people thereof when they pleaded for a king to judge them (1 Sam. 8:6–22). The rule of kings for Israel began with Saul (1 Sam. 9–10). His rule was followed by David, the favored king in all of Israel's history, followed by David's son Solomon, the wisest. However, the kingdom of Israel experienced a split after the reign of Solomon, in the time of his son Rehoboam (1 Ki. 11–12). This split resulted in ten of the twelve tribes, being referred to as Israel, the northern kingdom. The remaining two tribes, consisting of Judah and Benjamin, were referred to as Judah, the southern kingdom.

The kings of Israel were consistently wicked, doing evil against God's will. This cascaded from the rule of Jeroboam (1 Ki. 12:16–13, 34, 14:7–11). The wickedness continued all the way into the rule of Hoshea (2 Ki. 17:1–6). Within his reign, Israel was taken into captivity by Assyria. In Judah, however, ever so often there came into being a king who did what was right in the sight of the Lord. Of the twenty kings that came after the reign of Solomon, it is accounted that only nine of them did that which was pleasing in the sight of God. Judah, because of disobedience, eventually, followed Israel into captivity. For Judah, it was Babylonian captivity by Nebuchadnezzar (2 Ki. 24:6, 25:2). The nine noted monarchs of Judah that did right in the sight of God were: Abijah (1 Ki. 15; 2 Chron. 13), Asa (1 Ki. 15:8–11; 2 Chron. 14:1–2), Jehoshaphat (2 Chron. 17:1–5), Joash (2 Chron. 23, 24:1–3), Amaziah (2 Chron. 25:1–2), Uzziah (2 Chron. 26:1–5), Jotham (2 Chron. 27:1–2), Hezekiah (2 Ki. 18:1–3; 2 Chron. 29:1–2), and Josiah (2 Ki. 22:1–2; 2 Chron. 34:1–2). Interestingly enough, it is noted that the grandfather of Josiah, Manasseh, did not do right in the sight of the Lord in his beginning. However, after a humbling experience in captivity, he chose to change his actions (2 Chron. 33:1–20).

The leadership of the kings was greatly dependent on their relationship with God. Their governing of what was allowed, encouraged, and tolerated was based on their spiritual allegiance. Some actions strongly expressed individuals who were totally self-absorbed in their own agendas. Others proved to be fully engulfed in the practice of idolatry. Even though many try to circumvent the presence of God, it is God who is the sole source of true government. Beyond the kings, government was dictated based on the countries and empires of the captivities. One would see this in the books of Esther (Esth. 2:1–20) and Daniel (Dan. 1:1–12) as examples.

In the recordings of the gospels of Matthew, Mark, Luke, and John, the premise of justice appears convoluted. Justice and judgment seemed to vacillate between the priestly order of the Jews and the Roman government (Matt. 26:3–5, 57–66, 27:1–2, 11–24; Mk. 15:1–15; Lk. 22:1–6, 66–71, 23:1–24; Jn. 18:12–14, 28–38). This was fully evident during the time preceding the crucifixion of Jesus. The essence of this compound justice and leadership is noted also in the time of Apostle Paul, the apostle to the Gentiles (Rom. 11:13). Accounts of such unscrupulous proceedings against Paul are noted in the book, The Acts of the Apostles (Acts 18:12–17, 23:6–10, 12–22, 24–35, 24; 25, 26). The initial church of the New Testament (Acts 2:42–47) and times to follow dealt with similar dilemmas under different disguises. Martin Luther King Jr. would seem to imply that it all boils down to the mind and personality of a person. King said:

You don't see the me that makes me me.
You can never see my personality. In a real sense

> everything that we see is a shadow cast by that which we do not see. Plato was right: "The visible is a shadow cast by the invisible." …So I say to you, seek God and discover him and make him a power in your life. Without him all of our efforts turn to ashes and our sunrises into darkest nights.[18]

Beyond biblical times, one sees that the rule of the people of Israel, also known as Jews, the Jewish nation, etc., has been strongly directed by the rabbis, Mosaic laws, and tradition. Although there may be some compliance with the laws of the land, there remains a formidable allegiance to Jewish cultural guidance. Such rulings take precedence over all restrictive rulings of the land or geographical government. Alongside this, it is seen how some governments have evolved from monarchies to democracies or even a blending of both. However, Rome, which has transformed from governors and emperors to papal power, remains a most viable presence in leadership. Concerning this, Hurlbut stated, "The development of papal power is the great outstanding fact in the ten centuries of the Middle Ages. We have already seen how the pope of Rome claimed to be 'Universal Bishop,' and head of the church; we shall now see him claiming to be ruler over the nations, above kings and emperors."[19]

In light of all this in these modern times, Rome and the pope still have shadows of influence in governmental justice. This can be seen in the current issues concerning legal abortions and the reversal thereof. Modern judicial leadership tends to be swayed very often by activists and lobbyists. However, more prevalent would be the disregard of the justice of old, "eye for eye" (Ex. 21: 22-25; Lev. 24:19-22; Deut. 19:19-21). It seems hard to tolerate some of the rulings on crimes against life in today's world. Blatant crimes, some even horrific, but nowadays the judicial processing would seem to diffuse

---

[18] Martin Luther King Jr., *The Measure of a Man* (Mansfield Centre: Martino Publishing, 2013), 32

[19] Jesse Lyman Hurlbut, *The Story of the Christian Church* (Grand Rapids: Zondervan Publishing House, 1970), 82

their horror. Therefore, the outcomes of penalties and punishment are bartered out between the involved agents rather than based on appropriate judgment. The scale of governmental justice has proven to fluctuate radically in this land and season of history.

D. In the Church Sector

Looking to this sector, it is needful to bypass denominations. The general flow hovering over churches today seems to be one of laissez-faire. Whatever one wants, one gets granted. Here, leadership would almost appear to interpret church guidelines or revise them to align with what the popular majority desires. The popular majority may not be the larger number but rather the louder voice. Such guidelines may attempt to mar or overshadow biblical truths.

Yet despite how some seem to be conducting business, or rather behaving, there is believed to be a remnant holding fast to the "great commission" (Matt. 28:19–20). Within this remnant of church leaders are those who genuinely care for the Lord's flock (Jn. 10:11–14). Among those presenting themselves as leaders have been ones with their own agendas, and God is truly knowledgeable of such (Jer. 23:1–6; Ezek. 34:1–10). It is believed that in the church sector, if one is seeking guidance for leadership with biblical support, one should primarily search out the letters of Apostle Paul to his spiritual son, Timothy (1 and 2 Tim.). In addition to the epistles to Timothy, Paul's letter to Titus is also one for church leadership guidance.

One is inclined to think that modern leadership in the church for current times should incorporate more than one focus. Although the presbytery initially concentrates on guiding the congregation, there are goals to be embraced. The goals desired should include strengthening and maturing, growth in numbers, sustainability, historical remembrance, future leaders, and a legacy. The backdrop of these goals, hopefully, is embedded and tailored to the needs of the immediate local church and community first, and then the world. In the modern church at times, there can be a potential tendency to flow with what is popular or sway with the new fad. Some are swayed because of nurturing a desire to be currently up to date. Others are swayed under the pretense of modern so-called evangelism. There are those who make social acceptability a top priority. Needless to say, each approach or attempt has its merits.

Leadership here ideally meets the foremost needs of the people, in congregation and community. By taking this approach, the recipients will hopefully become more receptive to the message and transformation of salvation, the gospel commission. With all this, there is an underlying premise that shouts for strong attention. The premise is that the church is a business. Therefore, besides curbside appeal and goals, there must also be a system of organizational checks and balances. This is not referring to the financial, but more so to the functional. Just as one, when dining out, sits in the lovely dining area of a restaurant, which has all the needful components of excellent ambience and service, delectable dishes and treats were served and enjoyed, with a good time had by all. Although all this is good, no one thinks of the boiler room engineer, the sous chef behind the scenes, janitorial services, the suppliers, stockers, administrative and financial staff, etc., that go into this effort. Likewise, in today's modern church, there is more than just the worship service.

Today's church, in addition to worship services, may conduct a café, bookstore, credit union, school or academy, food program and pantry, and seek and operate government-funded programs, just to name a few. Alongside all of this, it may incorporate alliances with political figures or associates and strive to be a somewhat political platform or icon in the community district. With such resources and abilities, the leadership and church here may possess a sense of being well-established and successful. On the one hand, the early church comes to mind, thinking of when the needs of the widows were met (Acts 6:1–7). However, in seeking to be formidable or impressive in these modern times, the leadership of the modern church may find itself having a Laodicean essence (Rev. 3:14–19). If this becomes true, then the genuine purpose and goal of establishment and existence are totally missed. How sad it would be, that after all this, to be deemed undesirable, ineffective, and at a loss.

There is a variance in these times concerning the locale of some churches. Certain faiths and denominations are dogmatic about having only one church serve the needs of a geographically designed area and district. This may be noted in the Jewish synagogues or possibly in the Seven Day Adventist Order of churches. Contrary to this, there are other denominations or fellowships that are not organizationally constrained. Thus, one may find that there are churches of similar beliefs closely situated in near proximity to one another. Such actions may breed a competitive air in one's neighborhood, with varied churches seeking to acquire the same people and families as congregants. In this manner, there may arise frustration in leadership when constantly finding oneself vying for the same acquisition. Compounded with this is the thought of one's effectiveness being measured in the light of the competitors rather than the needs of the specific house of worship.

More prevalent today than before is the presence of the media. In the proposed strategies of the church, there has to be designation and preparation for the potential media. What is to be said has to be considered. Who is going to say it, offer answers to questions, or reply to inquiries needs to be, hopefully, designated in advance. Public relations skills may need to be groomed and enhanced. A projection of the image desired and its long-lasting influence and effect have to be carefully reviewed and chosen. Often, this is seen and handled not by one person only but by an interactive, strong team.

In light of the current events of this era, a major consideration for today's church is security. Today's society has witnessed an outpouring of seemingly lawless behavior. The sanctity of the church has been defiled with the infiltration of robberies, shootings, and terror. Some church leaders have revamped their church protocol in response to unfavorable potential behavior. Some have entertained security checkpoints and closed-door access methods. Others have even had armed personnel on board. The prospect of evangelism has become endangered. The "whosoever let him come" invitation (Rev. 22:17) seems to have become guarded. Church leaders thrown into this turmoil literally stand on different sides of the solution.

The church of today may also incorporate and/or employ staff that are not church members. These nonmembers are the helps to further assist the church in reaching its goals. In this arena, creative leadership may find or orchestrate an opportunity for evangelism in an unconventional manner and win souls. However, in this same instance, one must truly be mindful and watchful of beliefs and practices that others may attempt to filter into the standards of the church. The world at large attempts to be inclusive and accepting of standards and behaviors that are not always in agreement with God's standards and will.

God-oriented leaders find it crucial to abide by the true interpretation of the word of God and not the world's interpretative standards. An example of this may be found in the more widely-covered subjects being taught more prevalently in many schools nowadays. Filters and protocols need to be thoughtfully in place to prevent and resolve any issues. So whether the church has two on staff or two hundred, to avoid pitfalls and function well with a unified message, communication is the precious jewel needed. Biblically, one can see the value of communication with those at the tower known as Babel (Gen. 11:6–9). About communication, Lee noted, "Communications are the lifeblood of any organization. Without adequate and clear communications, individuals cannot remain focused on the same goals and cannot coordinate their activities for mutual support. In essence, most of the advantages of teams are lost if communications break down."[20]

Thus, concerning safety and all that may be needed, one may summarize as Solomon did in Ecclesiastes (Eccles. 12:13). Solomon says, "Let us hear the conclusion of the whole matter: Fear God, and keep his commandments: for this is the whole duty of man." Some may ponder and wonder why this is interjected at this point, but it is an expression. An expression of the sometimes hopelessness of all that one may try to put into place and yet come up short. If one looks at the general public and security for safety, professional policing is strategized and increased, and yet there is violence in their very vicinity. Therefore, one may conclude that if God does not keep and protect, there is no other no matter what is in place (Ps. 127:1).

---

[20] Lee Ellis, *Leading Talents, Leading Teams* (Chicago: Northfield Publishing, 2003), 158

Likewise, if God does not sanction the prospering of the program(s), it all becomes a futile effort.

As one may exhaust this section a little more, a closer look is taken at some of the many offices and positions overseen by some form of leadership. One that stands out is the area of worship. This would involve possibly a worship leader, a worship team, a choir and director, musicians, sound technicians, a chaplain or intercessor, and a manager. Leadership here has to encompass business and spirituality, as one would say, in a perfect world. Above all, as in all things, the spirit of unity needs to prevail most of all (Ps. 133:1; Rom. 12:4–5, 14:19, 15:6–7; 1 Cor. 12:4–6, 11–12, 14; Col. 3:14). The figures in this intense area must have expertise, a balance of understanding, teaching and sharing, and striving to bring forth worship and not just produce a performance.

Other offices of the modern church minister to youth, women, men, Christian education, domestic and foreign missions, community outreach, and counseling. In addition to these, there are ones that need to be dedicated to finances, bookkeeping, keeping records of events, administrative duties, and more. With the different amenities being offered in today's churches, one may ponder if the congregation and community are really being reached. The question of thought is, "Does the purpose of the church remain clearly defined?" Should the response to such a question veer to the negative, then action is required. Leadership has the immediate duty to skillfully steer all within its realm back onto the right course. This truly can only be done through and with the help of God (Phil. 2:13). In the milestones made, it is good to have remembrance in some form or another. Whether benchmarks, landmarks, chronicles, etc., these help in the continuity of the historical story being told and evolving (Josh. 4:1–24). The generations following will hopefully thus come to know the steps of faith or strategy that were taken by their ancestors, precedents, or predecessors.

E. Christian Leadership

This form of leadership has to answer to a higher calling. The true participants here know that the established guidebook, the Bible, does not change. It remains relevant and applicable in every time frame and circumstance. No matter seed time or harvest, wartime or peace, it stands. In wellness or dwelling in the midst of a pandemic, its beams shine forth. There are sound doctrines and guidelines to cherish and apply. The figures that operate in this arena are often called, and some, in the extreme, are chosen (Matt. 22:14; Eph. 4:11–12). Damazio writes, "Not only does every Christian have a unique calling, but each is called in a unique way. This is especially true of God's leaders. The Bible provides a long list of leaders who were called in a unique fashion."[21]

Christian leaders in this day and time have found ways to reach people beyond the church doors. In the instance when even the churches were ordered not to gather, alternative means were created via media, conference calling, Zoom, etc. These changes catapulted some into evangelical spheres that they hadn't attempted prior to pandemic living. In these times, an opportunity presented itself to denote those who were committed to the gospel goal and those who were not. The need and cry are still present to share the gospel, compounded with meeting the needs of care. Some leaders have partnered with others to provide pantry items. Others have reached out to those who are socially isolated with mailings and visits when and where possible. The work of the gospel goes on.

Having said all this, one abruptly puts the brakes on and asks, "What is a Christian?" By answering this question, the relevancy of what has been previously stated makes sense. Surely one would think that the answer is clear-cut and black and white. Thus, they are clearly defined as those who were first called Christians in Antioch (Acts 11:21–26). However, in this day and time, one might ponder if the answer is still clear-cut and black and white, or rather, a hue

---

[21] Frank Damazio, *The Making of a Leader* (Portland: City Christian Publishing, 1988), 53

of colors from the spectrum. Dictionaries in themselves offer mildly varied meanings. Nevertheless, the root of defining understanding would have to be that a Christian is one who believes the teachings of Jesus Christ and receives Him (Matt. 10:40; Mk. 16:15–16; Jn. 1:12–14, 3:15–18; Acts 2:38, 16:30–32).

Over time, the understanding has somewhat retained its original framework. However, there has been an evolvement of doctrinal diffusion, yielding many templates for who or what is considered a Christian. As a result, many denominations have come into being. Although they are all "Christians," what they deem as the right order of protocol may widely differ. Therefore, the leadership may utilize tactics that grasp, embrace, refuse, circumvent, or permissively allow certain practices.

There are denominations named as follows: Orthodox, Lutheran, Anglican, also known or referenced as Episcopal, Presbyterian, Methodist, Charismatic, Congregational, Baptist, Churches of Christ, Assemblies of God, Adventist (Seventh-Day), Pentecostal, Church of God in Christ, and Oneness, just to name some. Some of these came into being as a result of the Reformation Era (ca. 1517). Others came into being because of tyranny or even enlightenment. Some hold baptism as a necessary element; others do not. Others strongly believe in the practice of the holy Eucharist, also known as communion. Some hold fast to the seventh-day Sabbath for formal worship services. Others have chosen the first day of the week as the formal day of worship. Some hold dear and embrace the evidence of speaking in tongues as compliance with the Apostles' doctrine. Others do not consider tongues a vital part of worship or belief. Additionally, others consider the speaking of tongues a baptism of the Holy Ghost (Mk. 16:17; Acts 2:1–4, 4:30–31, 19:1–6).

From all these fragments and much more, one arrives at what is viewed as Christian leadership in this day and time. The true essence of this is to move beyond these isms and schisms and lead with a single focus toward God's glory. As one searches the Holy Scriptures, it is evident that similar issues arose even then. Jesus was noted in the Scriptures for addressing the scribes and Pharisees concerning their criticism of His disciples (Matt. 15:1–20). Likewise, Paul, in his Epistle to the Romans, had occasion and necessity to redirect the focus of the audience to whom he was writing. The focus is not on whether one consumes meat or drink but rather on the true kingdom of God (Rom. 14:12–23). The kingdom of God is the state of righteousness, which fosters peace and dwells in the joy in the Holy Ghost. Thus, and then, it is and will be the spiritual fire within that yields effective Christian leadership.

It no longer matters if one's insistence is on the formal service with the robes and regalia or ministry in the simple format of a casual gathering, as long as the Spirit of the Lord is there and with power. Congregants of any church tend to imply when God-oriented leadership is being conducted. One may observe an urgency in the attendance of services. Besides this, the conversations of the attendees express the richness of the word expounded and the power felt. This seems similar to the ones that travelled on the road to Emmaus (Lk. 24:13–32). The behavior of the congregation will often reflect its leadership.

The congregation reflects growth, unity, a zeal for the things of God, and perfection, meaning the presence of spiritual maturity (Ps. 19:7; Matt. 5:48; Eph. 2:18–22, 4:12–16; Phil. 3:12–16; Heb. 13:20–21; 1 Pet. 5:10–11). This is the tendency when there are God-oriented leaders. Leaders who are not blinded by denominational allegiance believably seek God's direction both corporately and individually. What they bring to the corporate scene is a mere reflection of what is happening individually behind closed doors. For behind doors the desires of the heart may be revealed (Prov. 9:10, 18:1). As one seeks and yields oneself to the Lord, there's a passion and zeal that are awakened. The Spirit-man within takes on strength. New awakenings with dreams and visions flow from this intimacy with God (Ex. 31:3; Isa. 11:2, 55:8; Dan. 2:19–23; Rom. 12:2; 1 Cor. 12:8; Eph. 1:17).

Thinking of the power of this intimacy on the one hand, and the amazement of zeal on the other, one digresses for a moment to look at the account of Apollos (Acts 18:24–28; Col. 3:16). Here, one views leadership as teachable. A figure utilizing the limited knowledge that they have with such fervor, mixed with their inborn talent, and being effective. Yet already effective, he humbly seemed more than willing to be taught even more by Aquila and Priscilla. However, this account also has more to tell. The leader qualities in Aquila and Priscilla recognized that within Apollos was what was identified as "good ground" to sow into, as in the parable of the sower (Matt. 13:3–9, 23; Mk. 4:3–9, 20; Lk. 8:5–8, 15). When one chooses to always have that quality of being willing to learn, they never stop stretching, growing, increasing in wisdom, and so much more.

Well, back on track with the dreams and visions. When bringing along what one continues to learn and observe, new strategies are tried. One comes out of their comfort zone. For a youth group, one may stretch to do sampling, a different way to do things with positive results. It may even be refreshing to change the location of gatherings from the church to a café, restaurant, or gym for a new outlook. Visions may initiate the organization of a Christian educational program, which may start small but increase well. The leader has to find balance between theory, innovation, and true absorption of the fundaments of the word of God. The keys to daily living are found within this combo. Christian leaders have a sincere and passionate desire to be relevant to each group represented in the church's community and beyond. Some may believe that they lose sleep at times because of the revelations that they get in the midnight hours.

Whereas all that has been spoken of is good and, to some extent, informative, there yet seems to be a part of this thing that does not always get attention. The part is the personal side. That part of life that makes up one's day-to-day. However, in this walk, if one will lend themselves, they will find that the rigid structure of one's day will be restructured and totally redirected. How one simply reacts and responds to the changes in their plans, especially the unscheduled ones, reflects the progress of the vessel on the potter's wheel (Jer. 18:2–4). Thinking of this, one thinks of those days when the plan is for total personal relaxation and the inner man hollers, "I don't want to," but there's a need and someone is pleading for your help (Lk. 11:5–10). The leader within moves with Christ's love in one's heart, and the need is thus met. Issues like this bring out one's willingness to serve.

When one thinks of serving, it can be, as Paul etched, that the leader preaches one thing but then falls short (1 Cor. 9:22–27). Truly, faith without works is useless (Jas. 2:14–26). The growth and building of a ministry are not necessarily measured in square footage. The growth and building may possibly be measured in the people. Measured in the ones whom your presence and input have impacted. One's impact may be in accompanying a dear one to an appointment, whether medical or academic, to advocate for them. Also sometimes to ensure that they are not railroaded into something that should be avoided. One's presence lets the person know that someone, like you, cares. One's presence also gives evidence to others that this individual is valuable and treasured by someone and thus should be handled with excellence. Caring is an investment in God's flock (Matt. 6:1–4; Lk. 16:10–12). Many things are spoken, but actions very often speak much louder than words (2 Cor. 3:2–3).

Life gives one many teachable examples throughout our daily living. In the voiced words of a now-adult individual crying tears, one takes notice. Expression here stresses that one has no clue about the tremendous positive impact he or she had on their life in earlier years when they were in a dark place. The seeds sown just seemed to be everyday or weekly efforts of mild significance, but to the recipient, they turned out to be so much more. In dealing with youth, being supportive of a good venture may have ripples that reach farther than anyone can imagine. The need is not just limited to support but also to consistency, innovation, empathy, and compassion, among much more. This needs to be strongly iterated again and again.

When dealing with youth, an underlying thought sometimes looms in their minds. The thought is that this leader will give up and leave, like many before. This predisposes to the actions of the youth not taking them seriously or giving them their wholehearted effort. Some of these tender souls (Mk. 10:14) have experienced unstable relationships with people coming and going in and out of their lives. Others have experienced people not keeping their word and not showing up when one is counting on them to be there (Prov. 18:14, 22:1). As a leader, one may be called upon or find it necessary to walk through the streets and visit the homes of their constituents. By doing so, one may truly comprehend the life a child or person returns to once they leave the confines of the church. With empathetic compassion, one can then be even more motivated to be diligent in their endeavors.

Beyond the confines of the church, after ministry has poured into youth, when a youth excels, it is a blessing. This blessing can also be noted when secular instructors in their lives identify their acclaimed abilities and qualities. When such a youth is designated and chosen to be a part of an elite group of peers to represent in the nation's capital, many are thrilled. There is investment needed in this instance, but in another form other than just time. Some approach such an opportunity in different ways. In cases where the immediate family is not presently capable of sending them on, there are those who resolve to leave it at that. Thinking of providing some type of consolation, some might suggest to give them acknowledgment when the church family is gathered and leave it at that (1 Thess. 5:12). Then there are others who get righteously indignant and determine to "Let's make it happen." Let's forge through with all possible effort and make it happen, which it did with God's help.

All of this is good. However, it is not just good to sit and gloat but rather to know the practical evidence of scripture coming to life and fruition. These milestones in life leave imprints in the memories of our youth and others in ways that cannot be imagined. They build one's faith and hope. In practical living, the message resounds that even if one is in humble circumstances, there is no limit as to where they can go or what they can become (Judg. 6:11, 7:25). At this juncture, one is inclined to muse on the exploits of Gideon. As a leader, one might truly determine to launch out into the intangible and see what God will do, honoring one's courage.

Even as the men of Gideon's three hundred lapped at the water with expectancy and were ready to mobilize in an instance, so one should function. Be in a state of readiness and expectancy of God's moving, opening up whatever Red Sea is before us (Ex. 14: 13–31; Eph. 3:20). Steward and Mann have stated, "At times, however, we all struggle to keep going. Too many obstacles get in our way, and circumstances close in on us in ways that leave us feeling powerless to change them. Some battles seem more pervasive than others."[22] In setting an example for the youth, as well as laying down milestones for ourselves, these struggles and the testing help us to grow in faith. Not only in faith but in tenacity. The tenacity as seen in Jacob when he wrestled with the angel (Gen. 32:24–30). This same tenacity is the one that was evident in Ruth (Ruth 1:16–18) and in Elisha (2 Ki. 2:6–11).

Thus, the core of Christian leadership would seem to be faith in all of its facets—the faith that is spoken of in reference to Abraham (Gen. 15:1–6; Heb. 11). This faith is first based on believing that God exists, then on believing and receiving Him as Savior and King of one's life. Consequently, to then exercise such faith as Peter and step out of the boat (Matt. 14:22–29). One needs to possess the faith of Joshua and Caleb when faced with conquering the promised land (Num. 13–14, 13:30). Once the seed of faith is planted in good ground, it has the capacity to yield abundantly to whatever may be asked or thought.

---

[22] Steward with Mann, *Leadership by the Good Book*, 161

EPILOGUE

As I have tapped on this subject of leadership, I truly hope that you, dear reader, have found it to be an interesting journey. Perhaps some things are clearer to you now. My hope and desire are that you understand the delightful interconnection of people, circumstances, needs, and behavior. The tremendous influence and effects one can yield in these areas are phenomenal, as I have found. I encourage you to be diligent in your calling that God Almighty has or will assign to you. May you be truly blessed as you go further and innumerable avenues open before you. Blessings!

The shout of "Blessings" is not an easy, smooth ride but comes with effort. So whether the leader within you is shining forth from a young age or coming into being late in life as a vintage wine or exclusively aged cheese, there is a need for what you can offer and bring to the table. It is absolutely necessary for one to establish in their mind that they are unique, one of a kind, and in a class all by oneself. God took time to make you (Ps. 139:14-18). Whatever one aims to be or to do starts in the mind. From this human PC (personal computer) comes every thought that will ignite one's efforts. Therefore, regardless of the platform, venue, or arena, the product brought forth is generated from what is purposed in one's mind. An ardent example of this is noted in the personage of Daniel (Dan.1).

One may believe what is purposed in their heart stays secret, but little do people realize that it seeps out in actions, attitudes, and responses. This happens at times when it is least expected. Our efforts tend to be most observed not when people are seen watching, but more weightily when they are absent. The leader in you will thrive by being focused and having a plan to execute. This can be as simple as cleaning one's room for the day. On the other hand, the plan can be tremendously intense. The intensity here may involve many players, points of crucial interest, monies, and outcomes, all interdependent upon each other. However, one's gifting will make room for them. Know this, dear reader, that much has been invested in you. There are resources, talents, and networks within you that may not have been tapped yet. The book of Lamentations by Jeremiah echoes His mercies are new every morning (Jer. 3:22–25). Besides all this, the challenge is to go forth with expectancy because God has plans for us (Jer. 29:11). Again, blessings to you as you continue on.

BIBLIOGRAPHY

Brown, Randy. 2006. *Blessings of a Father*. Lake Mary: Creation House, A Strang Company.

Connors, Roger, Tom Smith and Craig Hickman. 2004. *The Oz Principle*. New York: Penguin Group.

Cornwall, Judson. 1988. *Leaders: Eat What You Serve*. Shippensburg: Destiny Image Publishers.

Damazio, Frank. 1988. *The Making of a Leader*. Portland: City Christian Publishing.

Ellis, Lee. 2003. *Leading Talents, Leading Teams*. Chicago: Northfield Publishing.

Ferrazzi, Keith. 2020. *Leading Without Authority*. New York: Currency of Penguin Random House LLC.

Gladen, Steve. 2011. *Small Groups with Purpose*. Grand Rapids: Baker Books.

Hurlbut, Jesse Lyman. 1970. *The Story of the Christian Church*. Grand Rapids: Zondervan Publishing House.

Jakes, T. D. 2019. *Crushing*. New York: Faith Words/Hachette Book Group Inc.

Jakes, T. D., and Frank, Dr. Thomas. 2021. *Don't Drop the Mic*. New York: Faith Words, Hachette Book Group.

Johnson, Spencer. 1998, 2002. *Who Moved My Cheese?* New York: G. P. Putnam's Sons.

King, Martin Luther, Jr. 2013. *The Measure of a Man*. Mansfield Centre: Martino Publishing.

Leanne, Shel. 2010. *Say It Like Obama and Win!* Expanded Edition. New York: The McGraw Hill Companies.

Maxwell, John C. 1998 and 2007. *The 21 Irrefutable Laws of Leadership*. New York: Harper Collins Leadership.

Nelson, Bob, and Peter Economy. 2005. *The Management Bible.* Hoboken: John Wiley & Sons Inc.

Norton, M. Scott. 2018. *Dealing with Change.* Lanham: Rowman & Littlefield.

Obama, Barack. 2004. *Dreams from My Father.* New York: Crown Publishers of Random House Inc.

Robbins, Stephen P. 2005. *Essentials of Organizational Behavior eighth edition.* Upper Saddle River: Pearson Prentice Hall.

Rutland, Mark Dr. 2013. *Relaunch.* Colorado Springs: David C. Cook.

Squillaro, Tish, and Timothy I. Thomas. 2013. *Head Trash: Cleaning Out the Junk That Stands Between You and Success.* First. Austin, Texas: Emerald Book Company.

Steward, David L., and Brandon K. Mann. 2020. *Leadership by the Good Book.* New York: Faith Words/Hachette Book Group Inc.

Tichy, Noel M. and Warren G. Bennis. 2007. *Judgment: How Winning Leaders Make Great Calls.* New York: Penguin Group.

ABOUT THE AUTHOR

Gaile Newsome has found adventure in opportunities to pioneer and blaze a trail at different stages of her life. Seemingly, she was set on the road of leadership from birth, being the eldest of six siblings. Life has thrust her into such a role on secular fronts as well as in Christendom. This is inclusive of decades of service as a professional nurse, youth leader, associate pastor, family member, etc. She enjoys relationships and fellowship with fellow and former coworkers in business and ministry. Gaile continues to actively serve as an associate pastor in her local church, known as St. Albans Gospel Assembly Inc. in St. Albans, New York. She remains a dedicated native New Yorker.

www.ingramcontent.com/pod-product-compliance
Lightning Source LLC
Chambersburg PA
CBHW020628160726
47991CB00002B/953